SPLIT WORLD

Moniza Alvi was born in Pakistan and grew up in Hertfordshire. After working for many years as a secondary school teacher in London, she is now a freelance writer and tutor, and lives in Wymondham, Norfolk. Her latest books – all from Bloodaxe – are *Blackbird, Bye Bye* (2018); her book-length poem, *At the Time of Partition* (2013); *Homesick for the Earth*, her versions of the French poet Jules Supervielle (2011); *Europa* (2008); and *Split World: Poems 1990–2005* (2008), which includes poems from her five previous collections, *The Country at My Shoulder* (1993), *A Bowl of Warm Air* (1996), *Carrying My Wife* (2000), *Souls* (2002) and *How the Stone Found Its Voice* (2005). *The Country at My Shoulder* was shortlisted for the T.S. Eliot and Whitbread poetry prizes, and *Carrying My Wife* was a Poetry Book Society Recommendation. *Europa* and *At the Time of Partition* were selected as Poetry Book Society Choices in 2008 and 2013 respectively and both were shortlisted for the T.S. Eliot Prize. Moniza Alvi received a Cholmondeley Award in 2002. A collection of her poems was published in Italy by Donzelli Editore in their Poesia series in 2014, *Un mondo diviso,* translated by Paola Splendore.

MONIZA ALVI

SPLIT WORLD

POEMS 1990-2005

BLOODAXE BOOKS

ISBN: 978 1 85224 802 4

First published 2008 by
Bloodaxe Books Ltd,
Eastburn,
South Park,
Hexham,
Northumberland NE46 1BS.

www.bloodaxebooks.com
For further information about Bloodaxe titles
please visit our website or write to
the above address for a catalogue.

Supported using public funding by
**ARTS COUNCIL
ENGLAND**

Cover design: Neil Astley & Pamela Robertson-Pearce.

This is a digital reprint of the 2008 Bloodaxe edition.

For Alice

ACKNOWLEDGEMENTS

This book includes all the poems which Moniza Alvi wishes to keep in print from her previous Bloodaxe titles: *Carrying My Wife* (2000), including two collections first published by Oxford University Press, *The Country at My Shoulder* (1993) and *A Bowl of Warm Air* (1996), which were reprinted in that book; *Souls* (2002); and *How the Stone Found Its Voice* (2002). Seven out of the nine poems in the continuation of the sequence *Carrying My Wife* published in *How the Stone Found Its Voice* have been reprinted here immediately after the original sequence (from My Wife's Return to After Escher).

A new collection by Moniza Alvi, *Europa* (2008), is published by Bloodaxe Books separately from this book.

Thanks are due to the Society of Authors for bursaries in 1998 and 2003, and to Arts Council England for a Writer's Award in 1999.

'Of Chairs and Shadows' (243) was commissioned by the artist Eileen Hogan. 'Immortals' (284) is indebted to an article by A.C. Grayling in *The Guardian*. The quotation on page 203 is taken from Fernando Pessoa's 'If, after I die, they want to write my biography', from *Poems of Fernando Pessoa*, translated by Edwin Honig & Susan M. Brown (City Lights Books). The camel and quotation in 'Alamgir Hashmi's Camel' (270) are from Alamgir Hashmi's poem 'America is a Punjabi Word' in his collection *The Ramazan Libation* (Arc).

CONTENTS

Carrying My Wife (2000)

Souls (2002)

THE FURTHER ADVENTURES OF THE SOULS

How the Stone Found Its Voice (2005)

THE COUNTRY AT MY SHOULDER

(1993)

I Was Raised in a Glove Compartment

I was raised in a glove compartment.
The gloves held out limp fingers –

in the dark I touched them.
I bumped against the First Aid tin,

and rolled on notepads and maps.
I never saw my mother's face –

sometimes
her gloved hand would reach for me.

I existed in the quiet – I listened
for the sound of the engine.

Pilgrimage

On that dreamy late afternoon
the bushes alive with cabbage whites
Tom led me down the tangled pathway
between the mysteries of back gardens
and the top of the railway bank
where we were not supposed to play.

At last he pointed out a clearing
a sandy dip in the bank
and there it lay
a long fat turd.
It was Neil, Tom said.
Neil did it.
Other children had arrived
so we all gathered round
in a wide circle to study it
and it seemed to stare at us
burnished rich brown
almost kingly
as if the sun enjoyed it too –
an offering from a pale quiet boy.
Not one of us was disappointed.

Someone tried to burn it.
One by one we clambered up the bank
and trekked along the pathway.
Then later, at the tea-table
I thought of what Neil had left
in the vanishing sunlight.

Neighbourhood

Next door they were always fighting
calling each other Mr and Mrs
the names barking away
at the back of our chimney.

There were families with bitten
trickles of children
who pushed prams full of babies
junk and little dogs, smothered
and dressed in baby clothes.

On the run from my family troubles
I'd sneak to a back corner
of the playing field to savour
a terrible garden through the fence
where empty petfood cans were traps
in the Amazon grass.

And once Jim Skerry
bruised with dirt, never at school
came out through the din
behind his back door
wearing a hard brown plastic wig.
He sauntered off to the street.

Hydrangeas

The hydrangeas are massing
in gardens cherished by aunts.
Grimly ornamental, by tiled paths
they insist there is one garden –
theirs,
and if cats dare piss there
they swallow them
in huge mauve mouthfuls.

The hydrangeas are massing
heavy as cannonballs.
Guarding the house
they hiss to themselves
secretly.

They'll plan their own wedding –
invite no bride or groom.

The Afterworld

When your parents are gone
you will wear a white dress
and lock yourself inside
their empty house.

Daily, you'll pace the hollow boards
to the door, where you think you see
your father,
and the tree behind you
will be tapping greenly at the window.

A thousand times you'll write
at a child's desk
versions of the stories
they still pass to you in fragments.

Across them spreads your long hair –
it is still golden.
But you will not own anything
except the sudden sunlight
shining through your parents' hallway
up into your bedroom.

I Make Pencil Drawings, Scribbles, Bales of Hay

I make pencil drawings, scribbles, bales of hay,
bundles of twigs, a bonfire with parts torn out,
rough shapes of a man leaning on a woman

who leans on a child.

The distance is a simple line they turn to,
a tangle of rosebushes, the signature
of a dead queen – all black loops and angles.

I Would Like to be a Dot in a Painting by Miró

I would like to be a dot in a painting by Miró.

Barely distinguishable from other dots,
it's true, but quite uniquely placed.
And from my dark centre

I'd survey the beauty of the linescape
and wonder – would it be worthwhile
to roll myself towards the lemon stripe,

Centrally poised, and push my curves
against its edge, to get myself
a little extra attention?

But it's fine where I am.
I'll never make out what's going on
around me, and that's the joy of it.

The fact that I'm not a perfect circle
makes me more interesting in this world.
People will stare forever –

Even the most unemotional get excited.
So here I am, on the edge of animation,
a dream, a dance, a fantastic construction,

A child's adventure.
And nothing in this tawny sky
can get too close, or move too far away.

Hill

The hill heaps up her darknesses.

It is too cold for me to reach
the top. Yet she is always supreme,

dropping the lakes to her feet
and brushing them with her full skirt.

She'll never stoop down to her domain
now she has the luxury of a view.

In charge of greys and green-greys
she structures the late afternoon

with inky threads from stalling kites
and the hurtlings of solo footballers.

Slowly, she discards all detail –
offers me her dissolving horizons.

On Glastonbury Tor

The short grass at my feet is blown by a tornado.
Below me, fields level out to clouded glass.

St Michael's Tower – noble and lonely
as the last chess-piece on the board.
How I could hug a man like this!

Red Ridinghood's Plan

One iceberg December
the air mauve with cold
Red Ridinghood's mother
struck out her own heart.
She salted it, she seasoned it.

Her daughter swears to her
I'll never do that to mine
I'm going to visit Grandmother
for you haven't seen her
since the day you were born.

Red sets out across the forest.
The moon blackens like an old banana.
The trees have nothing to give but shadows.

She peers through her grandmother's window
net curtains half-way up.
The television blares and howls like a wolf.
Grandmother watches unseeingly
eyes swimming in absinthe.

Red switches off the set
makes her grandmother and herself
cups of reviving tea.
She takes the cloth off her basket
and reassures the old lady

I've brought you my mother's heart.

The Garden

A plum tree swayed up to my window
stretching to pick me.
The path strode half-way up the grass
where it finished, straight and grey.

There were two grand flowerbeds –
the circular for sleeping,
the diamond for fighting
crammed with snapdragons.

I dug up moss
between the paving-slabs
so that ants might flow –
until I stopped them.

The hollyhocks were the grown-ups
watching me from the heights,
shaking their rough, flat leaves.
They saw me running to the hedge,

break up mushrooms sturdy as tables.
I asked my brother
to lie down by the lupins,
pretend to be dead.

Dream of Uncle

In that open grave by the villa
you rest on your side
in a well-tailored suit.
Your back still broad and comfortable –

far more solid than smoke
that inters itself in the sky.

You're stranded so close to the house
I am loath to look at you.
Though you haven't diminished
you rise like a hill.

Your children still spin down the slopes.

Man of Tree and Fern

I must stand –
   my tree-legs are thin and stiff
my erection is bound
   it's all tree and fern
my arms are trapped in bracelets
   sharp as crescent moons.
Bundles of sticks
   grow from my shoulders.
Someone drew wings
   where I caught my breath.
I was a man of rank –
   you may tell me anything.
I can see with my eye-sockets
   dark as sunglasses.
I am more alive
   than the sad face carved
on my upper arm.
   I can bring you pets –
little bugs like pebbles
   the water runs over
and quick snakes that whirl
   like catherine wheels.

Before I burn

   the lamplight will flame
in tree-shapes
   table and chairs will blossom
for our feast.
   I'll stand by our lake-table
and you'll jump up

   to brush crumbs from your dress.

On Dunton Bridge

If I were an anxious child
I would wait by this bridge for
someone, anyone to cross it with me.

I daren't look down, my head
would bounce like a ping-pong ball,
nestle in the wasteland willow-herb.

I saw a couple fight here – Father
clutched a sobbing little boy,
Mother yelled *Get with me!*

at a girl in neat school uniform.
They all stood turned to stone
like Dunton Bridge. And I froze too.

Meeting an Ex-Pupil on a Spring Morning

Mary Jo, schoolgirl turned dental nurse
is smiling outside the surgery.
The wind clears the sky over Southwark Park.
In the sun-whitened street Mary Jo smiles –
a man in a poplar tree lops off branches,
leaves shine like silver on the fence.

Mary Jo smiles as if composing herself
for a photograph. This used to be my dentist.
Mary Jo knows. Tells me she's been looking
at my records. And then she smiles.
I see X-rays of my teeth blown up cinematic
on hoardings all over Bermondsey.

The blossoming trees brush against them
and hurl their petals to the ground
like sweetpapers. Mary Jo smiles.
A passing woman fills her baby's bottle
with Pepsi. And the sun, like flashlight,
bleaches the morning to the bone.

In Newspaper

My mother wrapped my cut-off plait in newspaper.
It might have waved its tail like a fish,
but it lay there, dignified.

My newspaper hair is robust and thickly plaited,
though sometimes a threat, as from a pitiless
comb, edges towards it.

Occasionally it holds a memory of snowflakes
from a first winter, settling on it,
crunchy as sugar –

or a sense of fingers pulling it into its muscular
criss-cross, and within it the longing
to be wind-blown horse's hair.

At the bottom of the drawer it's a rope to some
nameless adventure, all secrets
tightly enmeshed.

Free from snipping, splitting, perming, it waits
long years to be touched in awe
and splashed with lamplight.

It's an ear of black corn, ripened in newspaper,
in my mother's room.

Throwing Out My Father's Dictionary

Words grow shoots in the bin
with the eggshells and rotting fruit.
It's years since the back fell off
to reveal paper edged with toffee-glue.
The preface is stained – a cloud rises
towards the use of the swung dash.

My father's signature is centre page,
arching letters underlined – I see him
rifling through his second language.

I retrieve it.
It smells of tarragon – my father's
dictionary, not quite finished with.

I have my own, weightier
with thousands of recent entries
arranged for me – like *chador*
and *sick building syndrome*
in the new wider pages.
I daren't inscribe my name.

PRESENTS FROM PAKISTAN

Indian Cooking

The bottom of the pan was a palette –
paprika, cayenne, dhania
haldi, heaped like powder-paints.

Melted ghee made lakes, golden rivers.
The keema frying, my mother waited
for the fat to bubble to the surface.

Friends brought silver-leaf.
I dropped it on khir –
special rice pudding for parties.

I tasted the landscape, customs
of my father's country –
its fever on biting a chilli.

Presents from My Aunts in Pakistan

They sent me a salwar kameez
                peacock-blue,
                        and another
        glistening like an orange split open,
embossed slippers, gold and black
                points curling.
        Candy-striped glass bangles
                snapped, drew blood.
        Like at school, fashions changed
                in Pakistan –
the salwar bottoms were broad and stiff,
                then narrow.
My aunts chose an apple-green sari,
        silver-bordered
                for my teens.

I tried each satin-silken top –
        was alien in the sitting-room.
I could never be as lovely
                as those clothes
        I longed
for denim and corduroy.
        My costume clung to me
                and I was aflame,
I couldn't rise up out of its fire,
        half-English,
                unlike Aunt Jamila.

I wanted my parents' camel-skin lamp –
        switching it on in my bedroom,
to consider the cruelty
                and the transformation
from camel to shade,
        marvel at the colours
                like stained glass.

My mother cherished her jewellery –
    Indian gold, dangling, filigree.
            But it was stolen from our car.
The presents were radiant in my wardrobe.
    My aunts requested cardigans
            from Marks and Spencers.

My salwar kameez
    didn't impress the schoolfriend
who sat on my bed, asked to see
    my weekend clothes.
But often I admired the mirror-work,
    tried to glimpse myself
            in the miniature
glass circles, recall the story
    how the three of us
            sailed to England.
Prickly heat had me screaming on the way.
    I ended up in a cot
in my English grandmother's dining-room,
    found myself alone,
            playing with a tin boat.

I pictured my birthplace
    from fifties' photographs.
            When I was older
there was conflict, a fractured land
    throbbing through newsprint.
Sometimes I saw Lahore –
            my aunts in shaded rooms,
screened from male visitors,
    sorting presents,
            wrapping them in tissue.

Or there were beggars, sweeper-girls
    and I was there –
            of no fixed nationality,
staring through fretwork
            at the Shalimar Gardens.

Arrival 1946

The boat docked in at Liverpool.
From the train Tariq stared
at an unbroken line of washing
from the North West to Euston.

These are strange people, he thought –
an Empire, and all this washing,
the underwear, the Englishman's garden.
It was Monday, and very sharp.

Luckbir

My Aunt Luckbir had full red lips,
sari borders broad like silver cities,
gold flock wallpaper in her sitting-room.
Purple curtains opened

on a small, square garden
where Uncle Anwar fed the birds
and photographed Aunt, her costume
draped over a kitchen stool,

the backdrop – a garden fence and roses.
Luckbir found her Cardiff neighbours
very kind – thanked them in a letter
to *Woman's Own*,

spoke to me warmly of Jane Austen
remembered from an overseas degree.
Aunt had no wish to go out, take a job,
an evening class.

Picking at rice on pyrex
she grew thin – thinner.
In my dreams she was robust,
had a Western hairstyle, stepped outside.

After she died young
Uncle tried everything –
astronomy, yoga, cookery.
His giant TV set flickers into life –

a video of the ice-skating championship.
Has he kept Aunt's clothes,
let their shimmer slip through his hands?

The Country at My Shoulder

There's a country at my shoulder,
growing larger – soon it will burst,
rivers will spill out, run down my chest.

My cousin Azam wants visitors to play
ludo with him all the time.
He learns English in a class of seventy.

And I must stand to attention
with the country at my shoulder.
There's an execution in the square –

The women's dupattas are wet with tears.
The offices have closed
for the white-hot afternoon.

But the women stone-breakers chip away
at boulders, dirt on their bright hems.
They await the men and the trucks.

I try to shake the dust from the country,
smooth it with my hands.
I watch Indian films –

Everyone is very unhappy,
or very happy,
dancing garlanded through parks.

I hear of bribery, family quarrels,
travellers' tales – the stars
are so low you think you can touch them.

Uncle Aqbar drives down the mountain
to arrange his daughter's marriage.
She's studying Christina Rossetti.

When the country bursts, we'll meet.
Uncle Kamil shot a tiger,
it hung over the wardrobe, its jaws

fixed in a roar – I wanted to hide
its head in a towel.
The country has become my body –

I can't break bits off.
The men go home in loose cotton clothes.
In the square there are those who beg –

and those who beg for mercy.
Azam passes the sweetshop,
names the sugar monuments Taj Mahal.

I water the country with English rain,
cover it with English words.
Soon it will burst, or fall like a meteor.

The Sari

Inside my mother
I peered through a glass porthole.
The world beyond was hot and brown.

They were all looking in on me –
Father, Grandmother,
the cook's boy, the sweeper-girl,
the bullock with the sharp
shoulderblades,
the local politicians.

My English grandmother
took a telescope
and gazed across continents.

All the people unravelled a sari.
It stretched from Lahore to Hyderabad,
wavered across the Arabian Sea,
shot through with stars,
fluttering with sparrows and quails.
They threaded it with roads,
undulations of land.

Eventually
they wrapped and wrapped me in it
whispering *Your body is your country.*

Map of India

If I stare at the country long enough
I can prise it off the paper,
lift it like a flap of skin.

Sometimes it's an advent calendar –
each city has a window
which I leave open
a little wider each time.

India is manageable – smaller than
my hand, the Mahanadi River
thinner than my lifeline.

When Jaswinder Lets Loose Her Hair

When Jaswinder lets loose her hair
it flows like a stream
that could run around a mosque.

Below her knees it thins
to a wild sparseness
as if the wind tugged at it

when as a girl she sped
across the formal garden.
I crave Jaswinder's hair,

coiled – dark and smooth
as a glazed pot, falling –
a torrent of midnight rain.

The Asian Fashion Show

It's a charity show – a diversion
from chat, chips and baked beans.

I usher Asian girls towards the few
rows of chairs in the school hall.

College students parade – young women
drift across the dusty parquet,
modelling informal clothes and saris
for special occasions, salwar kameez
so stunning they ward off insults,
silks that could brush against years
of criss-cross graffiti.

Afterwards
Ruskhana shows me her Fashion Folder –
Asian clothes, pin-ups,
photographs of Imran Khan.
She tells me where to buy such outfits –
the best shops in Wembley and Moorgate,
asks if I have relatives in Pakistan.

By morning she's found out from her dad
the price of my air-ticket to Islamabad.

The Draught

I

In winter
there'll be draughts,
my mother warns.

Evenings will be chilly –
I'll huddle by the fire
which gives off fumes.
My aunts wear shawls
over salwar kameez and
socks with pretty sandals.

I'll travel with layers of clothes,
the recommended thermal underwear,
and I'll look up at those huge stars.
A road winds back inside me
like the Karakoram Highway
through mountains, gorges.

What to expect?
Aunt Shazia waits on Uncle.
Her dupatta dips
as she bends and offers sweetmeats.
Uncle Ali is building a new home.
My aunts don't know about it yet –
they'll live there soon.

There'll be draughts –
everyone leaves doors open.
Gusts of stories.
Bandits in the foothills
held up Amir's car.
They took everything.
Someone died on the journey.

II

In Shah Jehan's garden
where children splash their toes
in pools and channels
I'll hear an echo of swollen waters,
the thunder of warring countries,
and I'll wear my trousers
which mustn't be too tight,

envy the trees – almond, mango,
citrus, mulberry – riotous
in the formal gardens.
I'll shut my eyes
so I can't be seen
in the towns of invisible women.
New words perch on my tongue.

In my dreams I trawl
towards a brilliant sun
with a burden of gold jewellery,
push down traffic-clogged streets.
A trap of bones
is set around my neck.

And the draught?
The great draught
blowing me
to my birthplace.
Will it sweep the colours
off the salwars,

the smile on and off my face
as I try to hold a house
of Eastern women,
turning it in my hands
in the Shish Mahal,
palace of tiny mirrors.

Domain

Within me lies a stone
like the one that tries

to fill the mango.
Inside it is the essence

of another continent.
I fear its removal –

but how much better
it could be

to take it in my arms
and race away with it!

Etching

(for Javaid)

All the sparrows in the black and white miniature
are golden. Other small bodies are eels,
locusts, zigzags and crowbars.
A pale wool shadow of a scarf is suspended
in the teeming air.
The boy, who might be a girl,
wears a turban, and has two black eyes
from centripetal pressure.
He knows he can draw elegance
into the tiny white cracks in his eyes.
He doesn't know what suffuses him
where chaos and enchantment
jostle like relatives.

He is in a garden
He is underwater
He has one arm

The Air Was Full of Starfish

She was born
with the fervour of a bible-class
a senator with his whisky glass.

She broke, she entered.

Her mother bathed her –
a bowl on a check table-cloth
bracelets chinking
scissors and knives on the wall.

Mother and Father sat in parallel armchairs.
Her sisters were flinging themselves
down on mattresses.

The air was full of starfish
the air was full of flying machines.
Her dress wafted out like a powder puff.

Eating pudding in the marbled pavilion
private as prayer
she was changing minute by minute
like the amber moon stuck up in the sky.

The child – the dreamer, the dream
running in a torn camisole.

Her footprints stay where she left them.

The Great Pudding

I would like to announce this great pudding,
the biggest yet, blended by mixer-lorry,
steamed in a stainless-steel vat.
The Prince has ordered his portion,
and the giant boiling dish –
once used to soften willow-bark,
is now on show.

Children roll the pudding
down the street.
It's so solid
it has to be broken up
with pickaxes.

The Mayor takes a crack at it.
Outside the town hall
the pudding spins
like a globe,
blocking the square.

Coins glint like fixed stars –
it's hard to prise them out.
It isn't burnt, or overcooked.
Everyone aims for the core –
the dark, moist heart
where fruit hugs fruit.

When We Ask to Leave Our City

They say

Why don't you instead
cut off your hair
tamper with the roots?

So we ask to leave the Earth forever.

They say *What! Leave the Earth forever?*
And they offer a kind of umbilical cord
to connect us up to the coldest stars.

We'll stay in our city
opt for decent bread
lean our unruly heads
against the wall.

On Finding a Letter to Mrs Vickers
on the Pennine Way

A bird with a torn tail hops under ferns
and points its beak to the wall.

A letter to Mrs Vickers is trodden into the path –
colours have run into edges soft as cotton.

Mrs Vickers, Mrs Vickers
you have won, you have almost won
a Ford Escort. We of the Prizes Department
are sending you a draft of the Award Certificate.

Earth trickles over it like a child's pattern.

Mrs Vickers, calling your number at Stoneway
we would like to tell you
you're in with a winning chance.
Don't miss the cellophane window.

It shines like a dirty film of ice.

Mrs Vickers, don't forget to tell us
all about yourself.
Then tread this well into the path
where the mossy fronds dart like fishes –

and the bird fans out its broken tail.

Housebreaker

I dash my fist against the white walls –
they dent coldly like ice-cream.
Smug as a conjurer in the quiet hallway,
my face grazes slightly in the light.
Busy in the bedroom, I'm spell-blinding,
cupping nightmares in my hands,
turning them into silk scarves.
I long to feel the charred paper breath
of sleepers rising and falling on my skin.
If they wake, I'll loom up in monochrome,
I'll tell them how to catch a rat –
dye an ear of barley blue, for bait.

Moonlight whitens the lawn. A drained
swimming pool. Car on the track.

Is that a guitar in the corner of the room?
I could tell them how the lute is played differently.
Downstairs I'm a strange bird in a classical setting.
I fly into china, make cool, surgical music,
slide on the rugs, skating for information.

The house I gut goes down like a ship in the night.
At dawn, like a conspiracy, it rises behind my back.

Afternoon at the Cinema

You are watching a film you can't understand
with the man you once lived with
who reassures you that he can't understand it either
but he supposes it's not supposed to be exactly –
what was the word he used?

The film – you've seen it before –
it was a mystery then, and now you've missed
the sheet with interpretations on it.
Perhaps you'll get one later at the door.
The screen pours out its pictures
mirrors swaying like water
mirrors shivering in fragments
to walk through, turn back through
while pairs of lovers interchange and
there are murders and crowds and everyone
is tumbling off the screen.

You are watching a film you can't understand
with the man you once lived with.
You're in flames and falling on a mirror.
Was that something that he said?

Pink Ear-plugs

She found one of Beth's tiny pink ear-plugs
in the bed with the grit and crumbs
sometime after she'd left.

And then she imagined her
in grander beds, a quilt
falling away to expose her –
a featherless bird.
Sometimes she saw her furred –
a leopard covered in rosettes
she'd slip from the bed,
leap up a tree.

Or she glimpsed her lying with someone –
a hand resting on a hand
to see who has the smallest palm,
the longest fingers.

You Are Turning Me into a Novel

I hear your pen sliding on paper –
my skin thins like a page,
my eyelids quaver like words.

In the great silent hour
you are giving me a title,
fashioning me, coaxing me.

When I ask myself Who am I?
there'll be readers
attentive

on cool afternoons
bending back my spine.
I am the Knave of Dreams

rising from the margins.
I hope you don't think
it is my life

as you hole-punch the pages,
finger the ends of lines.
You are travelling towards me

at the speed of an idea.
The words you posted
are inside my mouth.

You are giving me a white cover.
Somewhere in each chapter
I do something terrible.

The Fire-Walk

I fire-walked for you
at the World of Adventures –
except I was unprepared
no five-hour initiation
to develop my resistance.
I dithered a little
removing my shoes –
and then I was off
taking brisk steps.
But the coals were not
the right kind
or they were not
at the right temperature.
My feet were flat –
I made too much contact
with the flames.
I stood still, transfixed
on the coals
and that was fatal.
More than once I stumbled
but was impelled
to continue walking.
I was not like those
who are empowered
by a fire-walk
who lose half a stone
in a fortnight
or start a new business.
My skin began to melt.

No one was held liable –
not even you.
You gave off stars
like a sparkler.
Fire was your element.

The Bees

Her breast is a face that looks at him.
On a quiet night he's convinced he can
open it and riches will tumble out –
pearls, golden brooches, honey.

The bees swarm into his mouth,
settle behind his ears, buzzing.
The breast is a safe –
but there's no getting in.

Ladybirds, Icebirds

Show me the ladybirds,
their colonies glistening
like a bloodstream
over the rocks and snow
high in the mountains.
Let me see the plant whose
lid of ice prevents the sun
from drying up its centre.
There's snow stained red
from minute cells of algae.

Penguins protect their eggs
from freezing, desire
a chick so strongly they'll
incubate a piece of ice.
I could take an icebird –
beak, breast, feathers
in my gloved hand,
now my hair is whitening
like the arctic fox
in winter.

Spring on the Hillside

You coax the flames, choosing
the logs thoughtfully.
You're happy
as if a bright ghost of yourself
moves through the openings
in your wigwam of sticks.

We stumble down the valley
to make phone calls.
The evening sun
wanders like torchlight
across the trees
the agate river.

I have never known wild flowers
live so long in a vase
as in the hills of Llandogo
where the sleet falls like blossom,
the stone path trails upwards
further than we know.

The Bed

We have travelled many miles to find this bed,
scanned tedious columns of small print,
waited in queues at bus stops.
And now we think we have it –

but we'll have to get it home –
no one can deliver it for us.

We must test it.

Is it wide enough for a family?
Will it hold the tempests of our dreams?

And when we are accustomed to it,
when the pillows burst their stomachs
and ecstatic feathers fly towards the cornice,
then perhaps, we'll have that river
in the middle of the bed –

where in the ancient song
the King's horses could all drink together.

A BOWL OF WARM AIR

(1996)

I

And If

If you could choose a country
to belong to –
perhaps you had one
snatched away,
once offered to you
like a legend
in a basket covered with a cloth –

and if the sun were a simple flare,
the streets beating out
the streets, and your breath
lost on the road
with the Yadavs, herding cattle,
then you could rest, absorb
it all in the cool of the hills,

but still you might peel back one face
to retrieve another
and another, down to the face that is
unbearable, so clear
so complex, hinting at nations,
castes and sub-castes
and you would touch it once –

and if this Eastern track were
a gusty English lane
where rain makes mirrors
in the holes,
a rat lies lifeless, sodden
as an old floorcloth,
you'd be untouchable – as one

defined by someone else –
one who cleans the toilets,
burns the dead.

The Double City

I live in one city,
but then it becomes another.
The point where they mesh –
I call it mine.

Dacoits creep from caves
in the banks of the Indus.

One of them is displaced.
From Trafalgar Square
he dominates London, his face
masked by scarves and sunglasses.
He draws towards him all the conflict
of the metropolis – his speech
a barrage of grenades, rocket-launchers.

He marks time with his digital watch.
The pigeons get under his feet.

In the double city the beggar's cry
travels from one region to the next.

Under sapphire skies
or muscular clouds
there are fluid streets
and solid streets.
On some it is safe to walk.

The women of Southall
champion the release
of the battered Kiranjit
who killed her husband.
Lord Taylor, free her now!
Their saris billow in a storm of chants.

Schoolchildren of many nationalities
enact the Ramayana.
The princely Rama
fights with demons
while the monkey god
searches for Princess Sita.

I make discoveries and lose them
little by little.
My journey in the double city
starts beneath my feet.
You are here, says the arrow.

Hindi Urdu Bol Chaal

(*bol chaal*: dialogue)

These are languages I try to touch
as if my tongue is a fingertip gently
matching its whorls to echoings of sound.

Separating Urdu from Hindi – it's like
sifting grains of wild rice
or separating India from Pakistan.

The sign of nasal intonation
floats like a heat haze
above new words.

Words like hands banging on the table.

*

I introduce myself to two languages,
but there are so many – of costume,
of conduct and courtesy.

I listen hard as if to sense minute
changes of dialect from village to village
from West Punjab to West Bengal.

These languages could have been mine –
the whisper of silks on silks
and the slapping and patting of chapattis on the tava.

*

I imagine the meetings and greetings
in Urdu borrowed from Sanskrit,
Arabic and Persian.

I shall be borrowed from England.
Pakistan, assalaam alaikum –
Peace be with you – Helloji.

It is not you I am meeting.
It is a sound system travelling through
countries, ascending and descending

in ragas, drumbeats, clapping.

*

In Lahore there grows a language tree
its roots branching to an earlier time
its fruit ripe, ready to fall.

I hear the rustling of mango groves
my living and dead relatives
quarrelling together and I search

for a nugget of sound, the kernel
of language. I am enlarged
by what I cannot hear –

the village conferences, the crackling
of bonfires and the rap of gunfire.

*

My senses stir with words
that must be reinvented.
At the market I'll ask *How much?*

and wait for just one new word
to settle like a stone
at the bottom of a well.

Fighter Planes

I saw the bright
green parrots
make their nests
in fighter planes,
thought I could fly
and peck at little
bits of the world,
beat my wings
where I was born

try looping lines
between the hemispheres.

The Wedding

I expected a quiet wedding
high above a lost city
a marriage to balance on my head

like a forest of sticks, a pot of water.
The ceremony tasted of nothing
had little colour – guests arrived

stealthy as sandalwood smugglers.
When they opened their suitcases
England spilled out.

They scratched at my veil
like beggars on a car window.
I insisted my dowry was simple –

a smile, a shadow, a whisper,
my house an incredible structure
of stiffened rags and bamboo.

We travelled along roads with English
names, my bridegroom and I.
Our eyes changed colour

like traffic-lights, so they said.
The time was not ripe
for us to view each other.

We stared straight ahead as if
we could see through mountains
breathe life into new cities.

I wanted to marry a country
take up a river for a veil
sing in the Jinnah Gardens

hold up my dream, tricky
as a snake-charmer's snake.
Our thoughts half-submerged

like buffaloes under dark water
we turned and faced each other
with turbulence

and imprints like maps on our hands.

The Airborne House

Ceiling fans whirl like helicopters
as if this house is about to take off –

And it does!
Servants, prepared for smiling

are whisked upwards, clasping jugs
of salted lemonade – and this house

this bulwark against the sunlight glare
floats clean away, leaving in its wake

vying carhorns, chants of street vendors,
the gradations of Delhi poor.

Hospitable ladies busy themselves
while rocking in the upper atmosphere.

They tell the servants what to do,
debate whether it is better

to have them sleeping near you or not.
And the girls tackle homework –

in English (Hindi's not allowed at school).
Everyone agrees it's been too hot

to penetrate the shops at Connaught Circus.
Tiger, the labrador bought from Harrods,

trouble with his back legs,
stumbles through the airborne cool

and sinks down on the marble floor.

My Father's Father's Father

In this city I have aged thousands of years.
I am older than the oldest tree in the world.

There are homes here for ancient holy cows
but none for old people, nowhere for me to go.

It is good that like the cows I am prepared
to wander the lanes and alleyways.

I was here before my father's father's father –
I think I can identify him, rising upwards

like K2 on an early relief map of India.
He is so old his skin is flaking like leaves,

his hair is soft as dust. I take his arm,
tell him who I am, then we are old together.

We vow to bathe ourselves everyday although
we are so old, because like the city

we are hanging by a tough thread
and dead-looking trees

have brilliant purple flowers.

The Courtyard

Stepping across to a whitewashed room, you look up
and unexpectedly the ceiling is the sky, with a single
star, its rays like the spokes of a wall clock.
At once you notice there is plenty of meat for guests
at the long table, despite the butchers' strike.

Then drifting past the melon, the tutti-frutti ice-cream,
is it a child who helps herself to bottled water?
At the same time she grows and ages.
She speaks more than one language – each fades
like writing in air and gives way to another.

She gestures to a side door – to the wedding bedroom
silvered with tinsel and glass baubles,
bunches of dried flowers in wallpaper formation.
The bride smiles shyly amidst Western-style furniture.
And the child darts off and loses herself

in the dark corners of the courtyard,
the hills of washing waiting for the dhobi.

An Unknown Girl

In the evening bazaar
studded with neon
an unknown girl
is hennaing my hand.
She squeezes a wet brown line
from a nozzle.
She is icing my hand,
which she steadies with hers
on her satin-peach knee.
In the evening bazaar
for a few rupees
an unknown girl
is hennaing my hand.
As a little air catches
my shadow-stitched kameez
a peacock spreads its lines
across my palm.
Colours leave the street
float up in balloons.
Dummies in shop-fronts
tilt and stare
with their Western perms.
Banners for Miss India 1993,
for curtain cloth
and sofa cloth
canopy me.
I have new brown veins.
In the evening bazaar
very deftly
an unknown girl
is hennaing my hand.
I am clinging
to these firm peacock lines
like people who cling
to the sides of a train.
Now the furious streets
are hushed.

I'll scrape off
the dry brown lines
before I sleep,
reveal soft as a snail trail
the amber bird beneath.
It will fade in a week.
When India appears and reappears
I'll lean across a country
with my hands outstretched
longing for the unknown girl
in the neon bazaar.

My Aunts Don't Want to Move

They hug their house around them
half-underground in a deafening city,
hurry across the yellow courtyard
with its waxy plants and coverless bed
where no one sleeps, sweats and turns
by doors to secret, sombre rooms.

Their house contracts and holds them.
Its simple brocade sitting-room
where uncle, father, brother preside –
they face each other on the mantelshelf.
The Alpine picture, the dividing curtain
women draw when unknown men appear.

They revolve their house before them.
It turns itself inside out.
The ancient wiring, knee-high stoves,
continuous stream of delicacies,
the bruising bangles waiting in the drawer –
just visible on the brink of the world.

Shoes and Socks

In the vast forecourt of the Badshahi Mosque
my cousin pulls off his trainers.
I've never seen so many holes in socks!

The exhibits here are shoes and socks
temporarily abandoned by their owners,
a little hope tied in the laces –

Ali Baba sandals, business shoes
all precious to the shoe-keeper.
Azam's socks have gaping holes,

one for each of his teenage years?
And through them slip his studies,
political career, his rebellion,

his dutiful laying of the table.
Religion rumbles through the holes,
the insistent cry of the muezzin,

fears of what will happen to him if
he sleeps with a girl before marriage
and is discovered...

Those who desire to fulfil their desires,
or wish to free themselves of desire,
leave their footwear paraded on the steps,

each shoe a small vessel for prayer.
Trainers for the new world, the old world.
In sight of the towering gateway –

the earthbound shoes and socks.

The Colours of the World

It is time, almost time
    for her to leave her house.

It is not normally done
    for a woman to go out alone
except to the bazaar
    to buy rat traps or garlands.
She glows within her body
    like the model of the Taj
inside the Red Fort.
    She reads her sacred script
which flows like water,
    recalls her husband's words –
From my first wife
    there was no issue.
She yearns to place
    a block on cloth, strike it
with a mallet – one blow
    for each of her children.

She ponders the miniatures
    glimpsed in the museum.
The heroine watching
    violet, raging clouds.
Moghul ladies playing polo.
    While outside the rain falls –
the white, the sapphire,
    the blood-red drops
spreading into lakes.

She will leave her house.

She'll go to the bank
    and see for herself
how air-conditioning
    turns it into a palace.

She dreams the women
　　are singing, bursting
in the red-light area, Hiramundi,
　　while she rubs her face
against a map of the world.

She's a woman with modest dress,
　　but when she goes out
the men will stare –
　　she'll be conspicuous
like a Western woman.

The fullness of her clothes
　　will swirl around her –
when the colours of the world
　　rush out to meet her.

Grand Hotel

This is how life began –
with a Grand Hotel propelled
into the middle of India,

breathing fire and ice,
sucking in the world
and hurling it away.

All the living organisms roll
on the bed with stomach pains.
The bathroom almost gleams.

The carpet smells
of something old and fried,
though incense burns.

Mock princes hover at tables,
poorly paid, return
to shacks and open drains,

serve the invaders, oddly white
and semi-clad, armed with
sticks and cameras and maps.

Lahore Canal

As I glimpse the agile boys
plunging into the Lahore Canal
escaping the torment of the sun,
I imagine myself a girl here
one slow, stifling afternoon
inside with the shutters closed –
rather bored, a little mystified
picking up another English novel
which begins *It was a glorious day,*
the hottest for weeks...

Rolling

In my dreams I roll
like the holy man
who rolls two thousand miles
down the middle of the highway
who rolls for eight months
to a Himalayan Shrine.
In my dreams I roll –
a battered van follows me
girls dance beside me
trucks overturn.
I'll roll like a map
like a bale of cloth.
No one will turn their head
no one will say
You can't roll here.
I'll spin through India's
hundred millions
pass through my father's house
before he fled to Pakistan
roll through my family name.
I'll roll right into the girl
I might have been
growing up here.
I'll roll in the day and night.
I'll hold a scarf
taut between my hands
to steer through this world
of sharp stones, fine dust
bullocks like rocks
at the roadside.
I roll beneath advertisements
for Cadbury's Chocolate,
the road warnings
Life is Short,
Don't make it any Shorter.
And someone is calling out
How much is a shoe
in England these days?

My dreams, my bandaged elbows!
I'm rotating beneath the neem trees
by ancient monuments.
I'm wriggling through stars in fretwork.
And as I roll the city rolls.
Rolls through a vision of myself
in the undifferentiated crowd.
The shacks, the rag-roof shelters roll
the donkeys with their impossible loads.
And in my ear the small scrape
of the roadside barber's razor.
I roll past women
cutting cane in the mud
women combing long dyed hair.
I gather all the smells and sounds
like a shawl around me.
I'm revolving on my axis
churning like butter or ghee
whirled along by chanting

until I arrive –

Somewhere I think I might have been
but it's not a Himalayan shrine
and no goddess expects me.
Only the young and the old are carried
so I'll walk the last yards
and then I'll stand and wait
with everyone else.
I'll touch my bandaged elbows
very lightly, my headache fading
and remember only
how I rolled ten miles a day.

Where Have You Been?

My camera had been filled with the details
of moghul monuments, but now it put its nose
in the rubbish where the holy cow
and the beggar who walks on all fours
cast their shadows – it nuzzled plastic bags,
smelt putrefying fruit – the lens wobbled,
elongating like an elephant's trunk.
All the odours are in the camera's stomach
continually churning and swilling,
with the woman who sifts through litter
searching as if it could take forever –
for a baby, for gold, for edible fruit.

Oh where have you been, my camera, my son?
Oh where have you been my one-eyed young man?

Delhi Christmas

In hotel lobbies skinny Christmas trees
rest on beds of egg-white satin

hold blunt finger-strips of cotton wool.
Santa gestures like a tour leader

next to log cabin, jewelled caravan.
Piano and cello send incessant *Jingle Bells*

into the costly international atmosphere.
And *The Times of India* hosts recipes

for 'ginger hut' and marzipan.
Inhabitants of silent corridors – the workers

murmur Merry Christmas, nod and smile.
Fierce air-conditioning creates a winter chill.

Sunbathers, indolent, line the swimming pool,
while England floats contained, so far away

like a glass-domed scene with shaken snow.
Cliff-like in the cool night air

Eastern hotels tap lightly into Christmas.
English couples talk of cats in Abingdon.

Rainy Season

I scale the wall
walk the tightrope high above
the house where I was born.
The neighbourhood dips beneath me
and the wind blows.

Daytime the sky is white and cool
as a bowl of firni.
Night time it flows like a woman's hair.
I conjure up the rainy season, command each drop
set this house like an ark on the ocean.

O Maharani

There was a place for me in the miniature.
Someone had taken the trouble to sketch in

my features with fine strokes from a brush
of chipmunk's tail, and my clothes surged

with brushstrokes from camel's eyebrow.
Sometimes the scene reminded me of England

with English paperweights set in mirrorwork.
Mostly I heard the artificial rainy season –

fountains in the Girlfriends' Garden.
I slipped on wetness at the edge of a pool

to the amusement of Ahmedabad schoolboys.
Then India opened its immense eyes

and I stepped out of the frame.

*

It was difficult to know how to cope
away from the painting.

Although I grew taller and plumper
I was soon lost in the raging crowds.

I raced on and on to escape and
was confronted by walls of fortresses

corridors and inner courtyards.
At last I found a Chamber of Audience

and a maharani who'd designed
a tale of India and England

for a patterned carpet
which changed landscapes

as you walked on it,
and was at first India

which melted into England
and then became

England mixed with India.
A knotted carpet

that could never catch fire.
There is such an emotional scene

enthused this queen
When a newly woven carpet leaves home.

And she passed on stories to me
as she'd passed on costumes

to her maidservants
patchwork kameez with hidden pockets.

I felt the weight of her stories.
Take something back to England

she insisted.
There was a maharaja who took with him

Ganges' water for drinking.
Perhaps you'd like a set of tiger claws?

Or stay here, so far from home.
Be like the rickshaw driver without lights

in the dark and smoke and grit.
You'd get used to it.

Then I thought of my beginnings
and sang

O Maharani
I'd rather be like the miniaturist who works alone
Painting on rice paper, silk and camel bone
Polishing an image with a stone.

The Laughing Moon

I had two pillows and one was England,
two cheeks and one was England.

Pakistan held me and dropped me in the night.
I slid through
            yesterday and tomorrow –

An unknown country crept between
my toes, threw an ocean behind my eye.
I couldn't tell whether the sky was red
or green, cotton or silk and if it would tear.

I could see myself spinning like an important
message through a hole to the other side
            of the world.

I'd held out my arms to kingfishers and tigers,
I'd sipped each moment like a language,
touched something I knew better
than my own parcel-weight.

Shakily England picked me up
            with her grey fingers.
England had a cure for everything
stuck between the bricks of houses.

The continents were very old,
but I was new and breathing in
            midnight,

the laughing moon in its place.

II

Exile

The old land swinging in her stomach
she must get to know this language
better – key words, sound patterns
wordgroups of fire and blood.

Try your classmates with
the English version of your name.
Maria. Try it.
Good afternoon. How are you?

I am fine. Your country –
you see it in a drop of water.
The last lesson they taught you there
was how to use a gun.

And now in stops and starts
you grow a second city in your head.
It is Christmas in this school.
Sarajevo is falling through

a forest of lit-up trees,
cards and decorations.
Mountains split with gunfire
swallow clouds, birds, sky.

Under the Brick

Concealed beneath a wasteland brick
a creased black-and-white photograph
of coupling – and we'd retrieve it
on those everlasting walks from school.
We'd turn it this way, that way, unsure
exactly how a couple fitted together,
put it back under the brick, but each day
find it again below the steel grey sky,
the London Country buses passing.
We'd pause, speechless, tilt our heads,
while their missing heads lived in
another world, outside the photograph.

At night I'd dream
and under the gritty newtown stars
the brick would hold down our secret,
would press on the headless bodies,
the limbs and their arrested activity,
the flesh more cracked and creased.

The lone couple, untouched by moonlight –
tiny creatures under a brick
in the middle of the wasteland.

Houdini

It is not clear how he entered me
or why he always has to escape.
Maybe he's just proving to the crowds
he can still do it – he whispers
half-words which bloom in the dark
Ma ha ma ha.

Sometimes he feeds me cough medicine.
Or bathes his genitals in salt water.
Then heaves his body upwards
as if pressing against a lid.
At least he prefers me
to his underwater box, to the manacles
which clank on his moon-white skin.
I wonder what it is exactly
he sees within me?
He touches my insides as though
he'd sighted the first landplants –
I'm catching cloud between my fingers.

Tonight the wind whips through my stomach
over knots of trees and sharp rocks.
When he rushes out of me the crowd gasps –
and I implode from sheer emptiness.

The Illusionist

He saws her in half – widthways, lengthways
and proclaims she's his finest illusion

when part of her is somewhere else
across the other side of the room.

He prowls up and down the echoey stage-set
and produces a baby out of shimmering air.

Then he flies off like Peter Pan, and returns
with all her lost boyfriends, like the first

who loved to drive cars backwards
and the fourth, with pre-Raphaelite hair.

But next he abandons the whole adventure
to twirl a floating head in a tank.

It's bleak in his absence, her absence –
she feels that he's hijacked her soul.

Until he cycles back on a wheel like the sun
and surveys her with undisguised interest.

He kisses her, stopping just long enough to
explain how once he made an aeroplane disappear.

Women of This World

Some women of this world
have my fingerprints running along
just below the surface of their skin.

Some women to whom I lent my clothes
are wearing them beneath the skin –
linen, rayon, watered silks.

Threading in and out of their skin
like a needle and bright cotton
go my fantasies, my finest hopes.

I interview myself severely,
handcuff my dreams to a mountain
which seems to fit their description.

I am seeking some women of this world.
I have come for my fingerprints –
I have come to take them away.

Burial

He'll bury her in the garden bit by bit
an eyebrow under an orange bush
her breasts below the rockery
and lay her smile across the gravel path
go up and down with the watering-can –

So every part of her will flourish
and her scent will overtake him
until he tells the world to stop –
and something of what she is
will fall into his arms.

A Bowl of Warm Air

Someone is falling towards you
as an apple falls from a branch,
moving slowly, imperceptibly as if
into a new political epoch,
or excitedly like a dog towards a bone.
He is holding in both hands
everything he knows he has –
a bowl of warm air.

He has sighted you from afar
as if you were a dramatic crooked tree
on the horizon and he has seen you close up
like the underside of a mushroom.
But he cannot open you like a newspaper
or put you down like a newspaper.

And you are satisfied that he is veering towards you
and that he is adjusting his speed
and that the sun and the wind and rain are in front of him
and the sun and the wind and rain are behind him.

Moving In

I think within me there's a space
where organs, muscles, blood
have just moved out
and you've moved in
with your exhilarating bird
your honest stone
a chunk of land
a slice of cliff –
I know it could be easy
to turn inside out
then cautiously propel me
through the waiting world
where everyone will see
how changed I am –
and gazing at the bird
assorted rock and stone
not know exactly
what to say or do.

Our House

Our house will have a parrot in the sink,
a horse cavorting in the living-room.
A thousand animal presences will canter
through the unaccustomed quiet.
In this house we'll borrow one another's
stomachs, one another's sighs, and listen
to the milk which starts to separate.

When the shadows of my domain overlap
the shadows of yours, nothing will stand still,
even the pictures will skate across the walls,
their phantoms tilt and speak.
of ripened afternoons, unveiling, dying.
Our agile house with smeared windows
where fireworks explode off the computer screen –

Change is a tremor in our wrists, our groans.
The carpet rolls unswervingly across the floor,
the ceilings whiten like cool skies.
We've alcoves of sad furniture, a hall of jokes,
telegrams with no messages, and on the pillows
those strange frogs, smaller than their tadpoles.
We are too slight for this brave place –

it is eating us, then we're ingesting it.
Our tour of its rooms will never end –
the first house ever built, our vaulted space,
The House That Jack Built, House of Usher.
We creep up to the doors, ensure they are doors
then light as insects
frolic in the dustbeams on the stairs.

Afterlife

Like oranges we roll right off the table.
I am lost as a goldfish stuck in sky.
No news of you, but I cry out
and you appear, carrying a photograph

of life-tormented trees – how glad we are
to see our old stiff selves released
sucked down, and melting at the seams.
We'll make the mistakes we wished we'd made.

They say the soul might have some choice –
I could for instance be a taste or smell,
something sharp curled on the tongue.
You and I as leopard breath or song.

My Prehistoric Name

I'm pulling myself out of one of my lives
as if I were an old tooth.

I'm calling up who I was yesterday
and what I was a hundred years ago.

I'll hurl myself down like a wildcard –
sitting here I've almost ceased to breathe.

Now the horse is in the igloo
and the rabbit's in the stable.

When the horse bolts I'll go with him
clinging to the tassels of his mane,

trailing remnants of a street, a dialect,
my childhood schemes, and I'll whisper

and repeat my prehistoric name.

All There Is

The stars are spiderlike
drawn by adults
who long to draw
like children –
and these are the child's
unanchored rooftops, hills.
The moon ticks like a clock.

The woman hugging herself
on her firm bed
dreams of a gay man
she knows slightly,
boyish, thin and dark
singing the mellowest song
she ever heard.

Yesterday she ran out of bread,
ran out of almost everything.
And now this dream
with all there is to see
and all there is to smell
undoing itself
on the fluid side of time.

Story of a City

I could tell you the story of a city –
how I seduced it in the afternoon.
The silenced birds were tangled in its hair.

I tried to stroke its million arms, its domes,
swept off some dust and sweetened it with rain,
unwound the suffocating scarves of dirt,

pounded it like a drum, like carnival time,
watched it stretch until it burst
with rhythm, paint and revelry and song.

Calming the city, subduing it in my house,
I thought I'd store it high up on a shelf,
or slip it in my pocket like a pen.

I begged on its behalf – a coin, a stroke of luck –
then left it in the dark recesses of a shop
steadily receding to another continent,

retrieved its deserts, chasms, embryos,
its open squares and theatre steps,
observed its networks running in my hands.

I started to examine how it seemed to be
just stuffed and stuffed inside itself.
Though once I cracked it open like an egg –

heard the river roaring free, the named
and nameless threats, the interlocking worlds.
At night I lie with this uncharted city.

It turns to me and murmurs in its sleep
I need you. Make of me what you can –
my suburbs of ideas, my flames, my empty spaces.

Tuning In

Now for the morning story,
or in the afternoon that tale
of adventurous, practical children.
Ship ahoy! Time for a new mooring.

With no special interest in boats
I tune in to the vivid location.
Something disappears on the airwaves.
Tendrils of spring are twining

across the electromagnetic field.
Comedy bubbles up from the archives.
Some of us listen, heads bent
as if in search of a lost item –

until a voice whirls and grips us.
We eat it up like an apple.
We are the indoor people, all ears –
disturbance is detected from afar.

Leaves crackling at the window.
The vibration of tremendous journeys.

CARRYING MY WIFE

(2000)

CARRYING MY WIFE

Missing

When my wife disappeared
it was grey as a school shirt.
When she vanished she switched names
backwards and forwards –
her own, her mother's, mine.
Hadn't she been orphaned, adopted,
rejected, married, divorced
and finally wedded to the stare
of the planets, the anxiety
of the constellations.
My wife was a rare occurrence
and a common occurrence.
She created a hiding place
in the empty supermarkets of the moon.
I called her a thousand times –
first with a map spread on my knees,
then with a tablecloth spread on my lap.
I remembered the phases of her dreams.
She had crossed the border.
Gone to a stormland, a scarlet landslide.
I expect she walks differently now,
rolls from side to side like a ship.
Clasps that child's bow and arrow
she took from the sideboard.

Quiet People

My wife and I were quiet people,
I realised after a time.
But this wasn't to say
that occasionally
we couldn't swing
thunderclaps between us.
So we were silently overjoyed
when the great composers
moved into our street.

In fine weather
we'd fling our windows wide,
or stand at our garden gate,
and listen to our neighbours,
mowing their lawns
with grace or difficulty,
dropping clear notes
like plant cuttings
in the silver, bespectacled air.

Toothbrush

She'd set about exploring my mouth,
its channels, walls and minute crevices,
with an air of untried enthusiasm.

What were her intentions? I shuddered.
Stop! I'd cry,
but she'd be driving over silver fillings.

There was often a quizzical sensation
of my wife searching for the dark,
strong root of my tongue,

wandering in the ship's hold of my mouth
like a searchlight –
a little lost, almost stunned,

she would admit
by the extreme gentleness of my breath.

My Wife and the Composer

And then I saw them – my wife and Takemitsu
in the gilded Department Store Restaurant,
taking tea, talking and kissing.

Takemitsu, she was saying –
I have weighed your exquisite silences,
laid them end to end and studied them.
I have listened to the tightening
of your arm muscles,
the flowing and freezing of your thoughts,
the notions that fly out from you
into the formality of the world.

Then her feelings took over
and I saw her kiss him joyfully.

I slunk into the street
exhausted by their intimacy.
He is dead, I consoled myself.
He's been dead for months.

So what was her affair
with the music
of gardens, distance and solitude?

Religious Painting

On the day of our marriage
the angels were fearful and hid

below the unreal, stippled water.
The youth who held steady on a platter

the head of John the Baptist gazed at us –
and the ox was purely astonished.

Everyone stared through rain and snow
until the sky returned to spiritual blue.

My wife and I shared a fantasy
of an infant with long toes –

our eyes became suffused with ink
and the buildings bent away

with the strain of recognition.
As the priest read from a heavy book

my wife listened intently, swished
her peppermint green sleeves.

Turned from me to contemplate
the extremities of the landscape.

Fish

I envied my wife her nightly visions.
She'd lay each one proudly on the bed

like a plump, iridescent fish,
and ask me to identify it.

Some nights I'd even manage to trap
my own by concentrating hard,

submerging the net into blue-black waters.
I'd place my catch on the rippling sheet.

So we'd have our own two fish, almost
indecent, nuzzling each other's mouths,

soul-fish, awkward in our hands,
hungry, as if our lives were a host

of crumbs to gulp in greedily.
They'd beat their tails very fast

until we could only see the one dream
moving between us, or feel stirring

one enormous fish, with our own lives
grieving, joyful, growing in its belly.

Carrying My Wife

I carried my wife inside me –
like a cable car I pulled her
up the mountainside of our days.

I lifted her quite naturally
and I carried the floating,
prancing seahorse within her.

I took them both to the crossroads.
Stooping like St Christopher
I bore her – a slippery wave.

The hospital parted for us
strongly as the Red Sea.
I coaxed her through swing doors

which gusted to and fro
like our past and future.
She was sea-sick.

Sometimes she could hardly
remember who I was.
I only intended to leave her

for a moment in the bulrushes,
but she slept and slept,
hibernated like a star

gone to ground.
Then I carried her
to the ends of the Earth.

An Indoor Couple

It was as if a child had already been born.

My wife stopped going out,
and soon I stopped too.

Instead of theatres, cinemas, cafés
we savoured the slightly different air

in each room, ate different food
depending where we were.

We filled the house with sheltering plants,
painted a hedge at the top of the stairs,

made windows in doors and walls
so that each room could spy on another.

My wife had lengthy periods of thought
between the smallest of tasks.

She said her new self was filling
all the spaces in the house –

at times we evolved there together.
A perfume seller, coming to the door

told us the most fragile blossoms
were drifting through our domain.

I valued this time with my wife.
Although we were indoor people

we tried our boots on the carpet.
Until at last it was clear to us –

time had sprung up
as from a bulb in the ground.

Backgrounds

Evenings, listening hard
I'd catch a sound I could barely identify.

Sometimes it would be soft as clouds meeting
or the sky seeming to touch the earth.

Then ear to the ground I'd realise
it was our backgrounds rubbing together

like warm hands, or dry sticks
which would eventually make a flame.

Countries which had once owned us
quivered with visions of my wife and me

wandering through them separately or together
aimless as cattle – I'd strain to hear

our pasts at war with each other,
county towns colliding, frayed at the edges.

There'd be the rumblings of our adventures.
I'd imagine my wife, struggling up to me,

laden with sacks of haldi,
or sacks of our vowels and consonants.

I'd view all the rooms we'd ever undressed in,
and watch us throw off our clothes – hardly

understood how we managed to let them go.
In cheerful moods I'd see all the garments

my wife had ever worn – they'd be dancing,
the jeans, pinafore dresses, salwar kameez.

I'd hear all the haircuts we'd ever had chiming.

All Fours

My wife took to walking on all fours.
At first it was just an easier way
to climb the stairs – but then it took hold.
She found it natural.
Her great belly with its new life
hung free, dipping comfortably.
We still held conversations –
though she wasn't much interested
in anything above waist-height.
She'd come padding towards me, her hands
roughened, damp, wrists and ankles
a little muddy and swollen.
But she was grateful –
she'd learned so much from the animals,
how to burrow, to investigate, to hide.
Dismissing all household tasks
she'd relate to me short, bright
tales from the lawn.
I'd observe her resting by the peony
waiting for it to loosen
its silky, provocative buds.
She'd surrendered
all the change in her purse.
Though I felt her hot breath on my neck
I couldn't follow her far.
I knew our lives were in flux
like the sky's reflection in the puddles
she tried so hard to avoid.
My wife, tigering the air,
snuffling forward.
The sun warming her ears.

Man Impregnated

And I envied her the baby within,
tried to cultivate my own –
first with a cushion to simulate the bump.
Then I gained weight, soon became
a man impregnated with light and dark,
with violet, with the wrong food,
with small bottles of beer.
I soothed and patted my own bump,
felt the delicious fullness of it,
the groaning weight of it – until
at last I awoke with a glass abdomen.

I peered into it constantly,
saw in miniature my wife and myself,
upside down, slotted neatly into each other.
I had no morning sickness,
shortage of breath or indigestion,
but pressing against my ribcage
were the feelings I could scarcely own,
the rough creatures which fed off me.
I'd ask my wife to place her pregnant ear
to my stomach and listen to the trauma of the sea,
throwing us up as driftwood on the beach.

My Wife's Problem

Smiling ruefully she unwrapped her problem
from around her waist
and slung it over my shoulders.

I had never disliked snakes
but this one had a devious way
of splitting into two, and then four
so that the whole unending creature
kept writhing over me in different directions.

I never knew where the forked tongues were.
I could never catch the tails.

When I tried to return it,
it declined to go,
as if now it were pleased
to belong to me.

Well, I thought, even
a problem has its beauty,
its subtle mosaics, its coil of words.

My wife became envious,
and wanted to retrieve it.
I'd hear her in her sleep lamenting
the apparent loss of the problem
she had unravelled tirelessly,
nurtured for so long.

Like a love affair
it had begun – and ended.

Waistcoat

My friend is perfectly at ease
in my wife's clear depths.
I can't make out his face
but his glance is apparent
strange and intent
sliding off the rocks.

My friend, the red waistcoat
I lent you, that I never wore,
let me swim with it on
as you do,
over the coral
in my wife's clear depths.

Living Alone

My wife had lived alone for a long time,
and perhaps she was still doing so,
making a nest in her thoughts.
She would pester her aloneness,
insisting on its point of view.

In summer she'd bundle up her solitude,
carry it into the garden and open it out –
a blanket of the finest quality.
She'd attempt to prise the burrs off it –
the vastness of her life alone.

The Unremembered Dream

We sat there on the edge of the bed
hoping the dream might emerge,
float up from a pattern in the rug.

It had gone off without her –
like a bright transfer that had worn
at the corners, faded from her skin.

A nebula hung round my wife all day,
giving an impression of this dream.
Could she recapture it,

anchor it like a boat?
Would it approach her diffidently?
I tried to persuade her it would return.

Not this one, she insisted.
It's receded so far – surely by now
it will have found someone else,

rubbed up against her.
Run with her down to the sea.

Her Song

A bird mourns in the afternoon,
and flutters under my tongue.
I am reassured

that even inside my mouth
my wife is still singing

Crossroads

When I catch sight of my wife
unawares, she is often
at the crossroads,
the moon and sun above her
sharing the sky between them
like married people –
and she is twisting and turning
as she does in bed.
She raves, first to herself
and then to me
about what she did and didn't do,
and she traces in the air
the pathways of her life,
marking where she said no
instead of a resounding yes.
With binoculars she searches
the distance for glowing moments,
startling regrets,
and with her sculptor's hand
attempts to give them shape.
I watch her floundering
in possibilities, impossibilities,
and stroke her shoulder
companionably, to comfort her.
My own crossroads – I found them
etched below her stomach
where I lay my head
for seconds, even years.

The Size of Our House

My wife would complain
that the house was too small,

her elbow stuck in the fireplace,
her shoulder wedged in the doorway.

Our lives scaled down,
we'd stand and strain and heave

against the walls, willing them
to move – but sometimes

our conversation would sweep
through the hall, and the walls

would automatically swell outwards,
the doors widen. So much space,

we'd exclaim. Just for us!
Periodically there'd be no walls –

just the enormity of the house
we scarcely called ours

hanging above us
like a ripe fruit, ready to fall.

Lizard Tongues

I had the feeling she was grappling
with a completely new language.
Eventually it was clear to me
she couldn't move from room to room
without a dictionary in her hand.
Every word I uttered, she looked it up,
then mouthed it to herself.
Everything she said, she checked it out.
I go to language classes, she explained,
two thousand times a week.

I could see them all –
they'd work on synonyms for wife,
pushing out their lizard tongues
further than they'd go,
thoughts pricking beneath the skin,
hearts swelling, thumping in their mouths.
Hardly space for words.
Much of the time they'd spend leaning
their heads out of the high windows.
It's a help, she said, *to swallow bits of sky.*

Awakening First

My wife would always awaken first.
I'd sense her sifting through my half-sleep,

searching for a companion as if
behind one partner lay another and another.

Her pores clamoured for attention.
I'd hear her devising complex strategies

by which she could awaken second.
I could have poked a finger in and out of each

utterance and left a slight indentation.
But then her words would harden with despair.

In a moment I'd find myself leaning over
my wife like a story-book mother,

detecting with my rabbit paws that
the bedclothes didn't cover her any more.

Instead she'd be smothered by the difficult
enterprise of waking first –

tired of making friends with herself,
tired of the glittering morning

with its pungent smells.
From my privileged position

I'd summon those basking experts
who awaken simultaneously

like two divers who rise above the water
together, and feel only a little afraid

as they rip through its silver skin.

Gold

At odd times of day I'd find my wife
bent over a heap of my clothes,

sorting through them,
holding them up to the light

like transparencies.
She'd shake them gently,

shake the grief out of them,
filling the air with my sorrows

more precious to her than gold,
Look, she'd say, had you forgotten?

And there they'd be – the old grief
and the fresh, nestling together

for company in trouser pockets
or agitating in the lining of jackets.

My grief that would soon break out,
flourish, on our best days.

Loss

At last I was certain that with the daring of an explorer
my wife had travelled to the precise source of my tears.

Your loss is so great, she murmured. Then she was gone,
and the world had gone too, speeding like a train

to the other side of the bed.

Substance

It would happen unexpectedly.
A rock on the path would split open

as if in a speeded-up film,
and under immense pressure

a silvery liquid
would push through the fissures,

the most delicate hair cracks,
and run over the mossy surface –

a substance
not wholly mine, nor my wife's,

shot through with unearthly colours.
In such a way we fell in love

many times
in the course of our marriage.

The Lake

With soft tearing sounds
we pull the sticky
darkness from our faces

and clamber down
the slopes of the morning.
It's all in a day's work,

hurrying along to the lake –
a thought to rescue from drowning,
a thought to submerge.

Or my wife on the shore
turning herself inside out
with the patience of a star-gazer.

This is ours –
our hole in the ground,
our deceptive waters.

This private lake –
one of the few undiscovered
places left on Earth.

If I Was Forced

If I was forced to compare my wife to something,
if someone held a gun to my head,
then I would try to do so.
But I wouldn't want to limit the possibilities,
or find that she had grown old imperceptibly
and the likeness was no longer valid.
So instead of comparing her to something
I go into the kitchen and take
an aubergine from the basket.
Nothing is more beautiful
than its soft, dark, smooth skin,
and for a moment no colour
is harder to define.

My Wife's Return

She had brightened so much
I hardly recognised her.

Her eyes shone, her cheeks,
her mouth, her promises,

her bones glimmered through her skin,
and her heart flashed.

The sofa dipped in advance
to receive her.

I sat close and felt the force
of each of her illuminated seconds.

She had switched on all the lights
and it was my turn, unusually

to rush to switch them off, or dim them.
You have been absent for so long, I said.

I left one lamp lit.

My Wife Had Her Hands Full

in one she held truth
and in the other, sincerity.
She let sincerity fall, but
something gleamed in its place –

it's a lie she explained,
a glorious lie, a fantasy.
She'd walk around the house
holding them in the balance,

the truth and the lie.
The best she could lay her hands on.

Troubled

As my wife picks up the spoon
a miniature komodo dragon
slithers through the casserole dish
over the lumps and bumps.

I pull on a plastic glove
and quickly lift it out.
That was brave, she says,
and gives me a troubled look.

Could she be thinking it had been me
who put it there in the first place?

That's What I Mean

I witnessed it often –
a perceived criticism zipping
through the air, ripping off
her skin so swiftly and completely
it could have been a leotard.

My wife – flayed alive.
That's what I mean
when I say that I saw her undressed.

An April Walk

Do you live to write, or write to live?
I asked my wife curiously.
Well, writing is life, she began – and faltered.
The wind brushed across the wild primroses.

We looked down at a pistachio-coloured egg
cracked open and emptied on the path,
then up at the towering elms
with their freight of nests.

She would sit on her unsaid words,
warm them until they hatched.

My Wife's Stoniness

I'd bruise myself when I bumped against my wife
to find all her soft places had hardened.

No child could take comfort on her granite lap.
Her glance was a flint. Her words broke the skin.

She drove her slate car under the leaden sky,
kept a pile of rocks by the bed.

I longed at such times for clear, sweet rain to fall
on her stoniness to bring out her finer colours.

I'd wonder, then, at my wife's transformation
and thank the stars for her human face.

After Escher

A hand holding a pen
draws a hand holding a pen.
But I can never write 'my wife'
so that it matches her completely.

I place my idea of who she is
securely upon her,
trying to replicate her curves
and edges.

But she slides away from herself
in anger, or mischief. I sigh,
tempted to fling down my pen.
My wife is so rarely my wife.

She is not the woman I met.
She never was.
The cock crows,
the dawn whitens.

It appeals to me that this is so.

The Job

You have thrown the job to the stars,
but they return it despairingly.
They do not want it either.

You observe it jumping over the moon
more energetic than the cow.
It soars upwards – an ungainly creature

carrying on its back a freight
of appraisal documents and schedules.
It flies without you,

without your eyebrows,
your insight,
your frenzied anticipation,

your briefcase of improbabilities.
Wherever it lands
it will arrive on the dot,

or an hour or two earlier.
Open the post. Begin the day.

The Drowning

I couldn't make up my mind about my briefcase.
I wondered how the sea would receive it,
how the rough, inky arms of the ocean
would cradle its compartments, debris, papers.

I pictured it going down –
convincing imitation leather,
spilt paper clips, unread reports.
I kept gazing at the sun
and playing with the minutiae of sand.
It took courage, even recklessness to wade
into the neutrality of the waters
pulling my briefcase like a fierce dog on a lead.
And when I'd pushed it under it kept rising,
lunging at me, black and bruising,
sticking loose drawing pins in my legs.
I was surprised at the energy I mustered
forcing it into the watery world,
and the sadness I felt when I thought
I'd probably succeeded in drowning it.

I'd once walked upside down on the ceiling with it,
dragged it along the Great Wall of China.

Never Too Late

There are things you don't think about
before you blow up Parliament.
You are so concerned with the barrels of gunpowder
stashed away in the cellar under the coal and wood,
the rickety steps, the crates to shift,
you forget all about the phonecalls to return,
the memos to type, the papers to staple,
the thoughts you were supposed to carry
from one hemisphere to the other.
For years you believed you were an alchemist.
In time you became a firework-maker.
You toyed with firecrackers, rockets, starbursts,
drove the birds right out of the world.
You longed to blow up a sovereign,
a minister, to madden a legislator –
make decent people shout in the street.
Surely you knew you'd be tortured and hanged.
You looked around for someone to blame.
It was Catesby, you whispered. *Robert Catesby.*
You'd had a lifetime of detonation.
They invited you to the firework-makers' last supper.
There was always a sparkle in your stomach,
a star in your brain – the opportunity
to give vivid displays to a captive audience.
But you knew it was never too late.
Never too late to creep down to the cellar
and deal with Parliament.

Nothing Too Passionate at First

While we converse I am fully aware
of colleagues lining up outside the door

keen to appreciate your new desk.
The sun has buried itself in a deep drawer.

This teak sun cannot rise again.
At the window beige blinds on tiny chains

conceal the territory beyond
which is neither yours nor mine.

The land is yawning vastly,
and your desk, so much bigger than itself

yawns in unison.
It starts to brag routinely

about the heroes filed inside it,
its clean, uninterrupted surface,

explains how it is left alone
in the dark, but is fearless.

When you leave for an unguarded moment
it confides to me it would rather

be an ocean, a mirror, an earwig,
any damn thing on earth.

All it wants is for someone like me
to lean boldly across its lacquered expanse

and kiss it to death, little nibbling kisses,
nothing too passionate at first.

Just Go Away

It is fortunate that as an exceptionally
tall and strong person I was able
to hover by the building at night,
force my hands through a hole in the roof
and wrench free an entire office.
I imagined the outcry,
the endless talk at coffee-time
about whether the room had been stolen,
or had simply worn away – the pressure
on everyone and everything being so great.

The next day I set down my trophy
in the middle of a field –
an incredibly peaceful spot.
Just go away! I yelled
to non-existent passers-by.
It's all right. Just go away!

The International Stores

It was surely
the least international shop in the world.

I'd note the cheddar and the ham
supreme on the counter

like no-nonsense Anglo-Saxon parents.
But it was an emporium for tins –

splendid pyramids, more spectacular
than my grandmother's collection

stored in advance for World War Three.
The proud ranks of supplies created aisles

on the marbled chequered floor.
You could have got married here

in the sixties in the International Stores.
Your bridegroom would appear like a genie

out of a superior tin –
He would certainly be speaking English.

Mr Davenport, whiskery, and turning grey
through seriousness about merchandise,

would conduct the ceremony
from beside the weighing machine,

his hands like meticulous pink sausages
welcoming everyone, to the solemn

marriage of England to England,
the happy union of like minds.

The Other Family
(for Jackie Wills)

I stared at this other family
as if they were a clock
and I wanted to see the workings.
The only family a bit like us
in the town, in the whole universe.
A white parent, a dark parent
from Ceylon, darker even than my father,
as if he'd immersed himself
in the world's darkest substance.
And his wife was so pale,
like the underside of something.
I tried to envisage them
on the other side of a mirror –
their crushed sheets, midnight bedrooms.
I tried to hear their conversation.
I contemplated the children,
browner than I was, carrying
their English names like snowballs.
We hardly knew the parents –
I'd never seen inside their house.
But I was sure that as soon as
they touched each other
their hands would stick together.

Ranjit Singh

Ranjit would turn up on our doorstep,
always unexpectedly, and always
with a different European girlfriend.
He had the air of a Bombay lord,
not a garage mechanic from Wembley.
I couldn't imagine him, regally
turbaned, crawling underneath a car.
Once I watched him deftly twist
his river of hair into a knot,
then create a trim beard from
his wild prophet's one, with a stick
my brother called his beard poker.
A little later there was Ranjit
with an American-style crew-cut.
Then Ranjit twice married, living
in Interlaken, his modern house
stunned with light.
An inventor, my father told us
proudly. And he's taught himself
to play the jazz piano!

My father's friends did their best
to conquer Europe.

I Thought My Parents Were Married

not just to each other,
but to couples who mirrored them
in Beckenham, Feltham, Potters Bar.
Each household displayed its treasures –

Bokhara rugs made rich red pools
on the fitted carpets while
framed Punjabi girls, woven
from straw, gold on black

danced above three-piece suites.
Marble inlaid boxes shimmered
on coffee tables like fragments
of the Amber Palace, the Taj Mahal.

But each couple's Indian food
was always subtly different –
the combination of spices unique.
And this was a joy for us.

Blood

Indian girls started their periods
earlier, according to my mother.
(I thought that's what she said.)
And she mentioned Neema
who, visiting years before,
one solemn afternoon,
had sat by the rockery
and named her doll after me.
A graceful, ladylike girl, but
suffering early that unimaginable
drip onto something like a dressing,
known by its initials, worn
mysteriously between the legs.
Was I more Indian or more English?
I blurred, as I would forever
when my blood seeped regularly
into the outer world.
I'd even run with that strangeness,
awkward in the egg-and-spoon race,
or guard it in the struggle to pass
an orange hugged under the chin,
hands secured behind my back.

Queen-of-the-Night

The young woman in her bedroom
with her forest-heavy heart
feels as if she's trying to please
all the countries of the world at once –
Stand under my torrential rains,
listen to the hissing of my branches.

But the young woman invents
her own story, stitching it in the dark.

Parents reminisce about sleeping on the roof,
tell her how the miraculously scented
Queen-of-the-Night opens
its starfish flowers in the dark.
But they're happier now in New Malden
where it's cleaner, inviting
professional people to dinner.
They no longer take hot milk with tea.

The young woman views the curtains
billowing, first with duty, then desire,
wishes she could dance lightly
from one land to another, or launch
her life like a ship, out to sea, or further.

Her own territory –
a box of jewels, or fireworks.
A walk in the park. Silver leaves.

Once

Once your parents hadn't even thought
of your name – then, for the first time
it glimmered between them,

kept airing itself amongst
the nubs of light in the lemon trees,
knowing nothing at all of England.

Everyone liked it – so you started to exist,
impatient to make a small flourish
in a long procession of namesakes.

Mistakenly, you tried to impersonate
all those who'd ever shared your name.
Of course, it would be of no use at all

to possess someone else's accent,
another's cough in the depth of night.

Takeaway

Our customer has faith in our foil containers,
our steam – that she takes away as easily

as raindrops on her new coat.
But notice how her life stands still,

neither warming, nor cooling.
She is expecting something to happen

before the grains of rice harden.
She is waiting – for a train?

A baby? A job? For the new world?
She has forgotten what she is waiting for.

We must take her inside
where it is bitter and golden with turmeric,

lead her where our bowls and spoons
scoop up the indoor air,

and the sun enters like an angel,
brightening our sauces.

Let us take her in case she has a pain,
in case the menu is longer than her life.

Let's donate her our burgundy curtains,
our undefinable smells.

The remnants of our country.

Thoughts of a Pakistani Woman in an English Jail

It's true, I'm happier than before.
Here, for the first time I know I'm me,
not this man's daughter, that man's wife.

My crime? I had no choice.
This wasn't understood.

My own thoughts
swoop like birds around my cell,
almost slipping through the bars.

Thankfully, they are not
Asian birds, or English birds.
At night I count each brilliant feather.

This feather is my will.
That feather is my right.

Incident at the Zoo

The bear laughed.
She felt a prickle of joy
when she lifted her snout to the bars
and smelt the perfect human baby.
But this baby was not perfect.
His eyes were weak –
the zoo was a blur,
its hot colours ran.
So his parents held him
closer to the mountainous bear,
nearly to its wet nose.
The bear laughed.
She laughed all over her fur
and down to her broad, flat feet.
The bear's eyesight was weak,
but the baby wore a shiny little
salwar-kameez and waved his arms.
The she-bear shook
her flaring, scythe-like claws
and seized this human child
just below his shoulders – tried
to drag him through the bars.
Love and hate shot through her fur.
The cloudless Lahore sky shrieked
and the branches of the banyan tree
hung lower and lower.
The parents pulled with the strength
of all the people of the world
to keep their jewel.
But the infant was torn in two.
The bear laughed and flipped
the baby's head like a fish,
stroked his caramel arms
and his soft black hair,
started to lick this new
winter cub into shape.
                        Then
she stood on her hind legs,

shuffled a few paces
and danced as some bears
are trained to do.
She danced on air.

Arctic Summer

The summer leapt up and was gone.

We speculated –
had it been harmed or insulted?

Was it sinking to the ground
holding the sun in its arms

like a beachball?
Perhaps it was off playing tennis.

Or had it been entranced by a vision
of skaters on a frozen sea?

Once we stood in a golden pool
and were quite oblivious of it.

But now the summer approaches
like a perfect companion

who questions whether
we really desire her,

placing her hand in ours,
and pulling it away.

The Uncertainty of the Heart

We know where the heart is –
its home, its place on the map.

But today the heart hovers just outside the body
like a visitor who, afraid she has arrived
too early, is unsure whether it is
the rain or the sunshine
she should wipe from her feet.

The World Has a Passion

You hope something will blossom inside you,
    taking shape like a fresh thought.
Sometimes it is the progeny of sunlight,
    and then it is the chill of the sea.
Or you imagine you have seen the creature,
    blue and crouched like an alley cat.
        under the illustrious moon.

Now walking on water with ease,
    it looks up and addresses you strictly,
asking if you are prepared for it.
    It will travel to the most atrocious
places on Earth, where it will light
    an unsteady candle, send you a letter,
        or a mothwing invitation.

The radio plays stoutly, quite sure of itself –
    and life makes for you on the up-escalator,
whirrs above like a helicopter.
    beckons like a cinema complex.
And this is because the world
    has a passion for making faces,
        elliptical new faces.

    It sings and sighs
        over the faces it creates.

Bully

My body takes charge like some kind of bully.
It grapples with a monstrous head cold
and swells with deliberation,
drawing the sun's rays into itself,
guarding the curled newcomer
and leaving me with the sickness.

It goes about its business
itching, smelling differently
like someone else's house.

In the middle of the night
my body will assault me,
challenge me to a fight
like the girl in the playground
who rolled up her sleeves
and spat on her hands.

In the darkness
we'll tussle for the golden one.

Storyteller

Two centuries ago
I thought I heard a rustling
in my stomach – trees grew there
swishing gentle-fingered branches.
In another continent a small
puma disturbed a clearing –
even the sunlight could be heard.
Now that I am large enough to contain
all the noises of the universe,
the scraping of classroom chairs,
the siren's *waa-waa waa-waa*
you are there with no human voice.
But occasionally I hear you,
your enthusiastic half-life,
your incidental music.
And when you turn over it is as if
I am listening to a distant
but enthralling storyteller
turning the page
or briefly clearing her throat.

Giants with Tender Hands

The giants with tender hands
don't know what to do.

Should they wipe her eyes?
Should they do it now?

She isn't a lamb or kitten.
But she is the fawn
they must carry through the forest
on and on to where the trees thin out.
Like the elderly couple
who'd always dreamed of a child,
they had three wishes and one came true.
They'll stumble often because they
are the oldest people in the land.
They crack easily, like eggshells,
lamenting how all their wisdom
has been snatched by the north wind.

Their child, in a shawl of warm white snow –
she'll set fire to their house of straw,
kick down their house of stone.

The Old Woman Who Lived in a Shoe

despaired of her children –
fighting and tumbling all over
their cramped, unsuitable home.
She was relieved each evening
when she got them into bed
and the youngest stopped
tugging at the bootlaces,
and eating shoe polish,
and finally fell asleep.

She'd go to her garden patch
and revel in solitude –
she'd survived the day,
and so had the children.
In summer she'd stay up late
with the Man in the Moon
for company, and the astounding
spaciousness of the sky.

The Child Goddess

Let us suppose that we have given birth
to the Royal Kumari of Patan –

the child goddess who blesses
marriages, heals the sick,

and gazes just to the side of those
who've reached the dark star

of puberty. Our personal deity –
We are so proud!

She no longer pulls our hair.
She doesn't have tooth decay.

Perhaps she'll be seven years old forever.
Everyone stares at her vulnerable face

and proclaims she has the cheeks of a lion.
At times we despair that she is never

allowed to leave our home except
when we parade her through the streets.

The most powerful of all virgins,
she is only permitted one friend.

We dress her in glittering scarlet
and sit her on a scarlet chair.

She clutches the arms of this throne
as if she is about to stand up

and run outside and play.
But she is utterly still, utterly quiet.

One day, inevitably
she'll graze her knee, prick a finger,

lose a tooth – her goddess status
disappearing with her first drop of blood.

She'll become a little like a real child.
Our Kumari of Kathmandu,

of the suburbs, of wherever we are.

The Last Page

The woman climbs the steps of the church tower.
At first stone steps, then wooden.
So finally, just before she throws herself

from the parapet her steps are quieter.
But was it wise to end the novel in this way,
the narrative jumping off the ledge,

or should the woman have died at the beginning
of the story, the author slowly replaying
her fall – backwards, or perhaps the leap

should have occurred in the middle of it all
with the two halves of the book held open
like the pair of wings which might have saved her?

SOULS

(2002)

THE FURTHER ADVENTURES
OF THE SOULS

Presents

Come closer.
It is Christmas morning.

The souls are opening their presents,
unpacking their empty boxes
in perfect harmony with the void.

Nothingness is the most sensible gift –
it doesn't clash with anything
and if you have some already
it isn't a problem to receive a little more.

The souls hold it shakily on a spoon
as if they are ravenous
as if they are about to eat.

Don't Pity Them

They bring their own daylight
which they transport, folded

in soft white tissue paper.
Souls are renowned collectors –

they wait like indoor birdwatchers
in hallways and doorways

for lozenges of light.
Create your own world,

they advise. *Collect nothing*
which isn't infinitely collectible.

Don't pity them
as they bend over their scrapbooks,

cutting and sticking, rearranging the light.

Whatever the Weather

It's essential that the souls
don't make themselves too obvious.
Think what might happen
if they revealed themselves openly –
they'd be blamed for everything.

So they ensure they're harder
to contemplate
than summer in winter.
Whatever the weather,
how discreet they are!

Young souls learn to dress themselves –
wrap themselves in obscurity.

The Scene of the Crime

The set – a country house
with oak panelling, and outside

a blizzard from a melodrama.
An inspector called to investigate

the disappearance of a soul –
a murder by an unseen hand.

The souls – are they ever he or she?
Hot or cold? Who knows.

Perhaps, when they go
they're inquisitive, as curious

as those who seek them?
Do they leave alone, or could they

huddle together behind a sofa
in a snowbound manor?

There's not a single clue.
Just polite conversation growing

steadily more frenzied.
A door slams, dislodging

a lampshade. And somewhere
out in the night,

a soul goes off like a gun.

Without Us

Souls are divorced many times.
They exist as discarded fragments –
a name left behind,

an unfashionable scarf,
nail parings.
They are so light without us.

They survive alone
like bedsit dwellers
very close to their own atmosphere.

They can cope with this.
But a room is uneasy
with an invisible occupant.

   The landlady catches her breath
   and pulls her chair closer to the fire.

Travellers

Generally, they're good travellers,
well equipped – life's experiences
stuffed into their airy rucksacks.
The souls love skimming the tops of trees.
Though some flutter noisily,
protesting like bored children
Are we nearly there yet?

And what can the world do,
but put its hands over its ears?

Lost Souls

Lost souls are not always lost.
They inhabit us as if our faces
were portraits in galleries –

and stare out of us
until they are tired of looking.
We are tired too – boxed in,
exhausted with sitting still.
Eventually we get cramp,
backache, however sumptuous
our clothes, rosy our cheeks.

Strangely, when the souls
are tired of looking,
it does sometimes happen
that our clothes rustle,
our eyes move.

Who Can Blame Them?

And some are forced to grow
as fast as possible –
let's call them chicken souls.

Crammed into sheds
or shackled upside down,
they develop abnormalities.
Who can blame them
when they peck at painkillers,
or envy those allowed

to go outside –
though rumour has it
all that fresh air's rationed
and the frost
puts hostile feathers
on the backs of chicken souls.

Bat

Like a bat it hangs, and keeps on hanging.
Hibernating – or in need of help?
The soul is a vulnerable species –
and some get very worn, as bats
might have worn teeth.

The soul, hanging on out there,
on a wall, longing
to fit into the palm of a hand.

Immortals

The souls are continually hunting
fervent as hounds, not for a fox,
but for a den – somewhere
to lie down, set up home.

We feel for them,
because who would wish
to live forever?

But they're bemused –
we live our lives,
tell our stories,
ignorant of the last instalment.

We only know about life.
To the souls,
we're the real immortals.

In Space

When souls go into orbit
they find the food impossible –

bite-sized cubes, zero-gravity meals
and everything heat-treated
to prevent decay. Scissors
for snipping the tops off food bags –
the souls float straight through them.

They evade it all
and make for deeper space,
vow to consume nothing
but songs without words.

They mock us gently –
our brief space flights,
the music we try to clothe
with flesh and bone.

The Worst Thing

The worst thing for the souls
is forgetting how to fly.

No chance to star
on Prospero's island.

They'll almost grieve,
then lie in wait

for the moment of their
liberation –

when even the most inept
will soar so high and fast

no sharp-eared god
can hear them coming.

The Marriage

They get used to crowds,
huge, seething crowds,
surging down the streets
and across the fields,
filling the crevices.

No space between the blades of grass.
Not just crowds of themselves,
the multiplicity of souls –
but throngs of hopes and desires,

fateful endeavours,
joys, perplexities,
do's and don'ts.

The souls marry the crowds.
There's no ceremony,
though sometimes there's music,
muffled, cacophonous –
and the bells of lost churches

ring out under the sea.

The Other Room

This is the room reflected in the window.
Walk inside, explore it for yourself.
The fire is glacial crimson.

The walls are filmy, not like walls at all.
These are the most densely populated
living-rooms on earth.

But who lives in them? The souls
settle here in their multitudes,
visit the spines of weightless books,

the floating hands of clocks.
Sink into armchairs in the snow.
Lose interest in us, even

as they beat so fiercely
against our bolder rooms,
the glass of the world.

Beds

They can't decide whether finally
they are more, or less alone,

and can't help longing
for a real, solid bed,

pine, or four-poster, to share
with one other soul –

not the thousands
who'd attempt to drift in.

What do the souls do in bed?
Not touching exactly,

but a warm overlapping.
In the morning they descend

the stairs, separate from the world
but only slightly

like a girl who has just
washed her hair, and they

assure themselves that after all
they are a marvellous invention.

Family Reunions

Just when they think they've made it –
the shock
of numberless, faceless relatives
filling up infinity.

Awkward meetings.
Parties with invisible food and drink.
Embarrassed shiftings
take the place of dancing.

Family reunions are overwhelming
for the souls.
The semi-familiar billions.
No getaway car.

Nowhere else to go.

Escape

The souls are playing truant,
escaping the strain of us,
finding places to hide –

in lifts and murky stairwells,
under bridges. Up there
with the pigeons, they glance

down and marvel at
how hard we try to tell one
soul from another, the boxes

we force them in, the countries
we try to pin on them.
But they won't have it.

However hard we press down
on the lid, out they come,
out of the box.

The Directors

They're busiest at night,
fiddling with the roots of our hair,
stroking the backs of our eyes,
setting in motion the nightly film.

As the dream gathers its singular
momentum, the souls burrow
into our bones, circle
just above our heads...

Then one night the dream slips
away from them, fizzles out.
So what can they do when
we've skidded into their past?

The directors of nothing.
Did we give up on them,
or them on us?

Shirt on the Line

The souls are not always serious.
It is such fun for them
to inhabit the shirt on the line.

The white shirt, usually so proper –
tucked in and belted into place.
The soul, like the wind

fills out the chest,
and the sleeves are riotous,
swaying and flapping.

The empty shirt is a joy –
for an hour the souls forget
what they carry with them,

have no idea whether
it is a happy childhood,
or a great weariness.

A Soul is Showing

Sometimes a soul is showing.

You can glimpse it like a slip
hanging an inch below a skirt.

You see it,
         then your friend sees it,
                           your neighbour,
the man at the corner shop.

And even those at a great distance
seem to perceive it –

the lighthouse keeper,
so used to the souls
repeating themselves
on the tips of waves.

Perhaps it's not such a big deal.
No need to be embarrassed
because a soul is showing.

Quiet Work

So much time spent
hovering inside us, uncomplainingly.
Their quiet work is never done –

the slow linking of our past's past
to our future's future
with no elaborate equipment.

How different the souls are
from the beleaguered memory,
stalking through a lost empire,

excited about the catch of the day,
fingering the stolen goods.

Even the Sun

Expanding souls shoot upwards, outwards,
persuade us to extend their homes,
make balconies, rooms in the roof,
more space for guests.
To them, so much is possible –

even the moon could call them up,
even the sun could stay the night.

Great and Small

The second is the great thing,
not the years, the days,
the protracted minutes.
The souls know so well
the particles of time,
their scent,
their explosive nature.

If there's a special vibrancy,
or a stillness in the air,
it could be the souls
protecting the seconds,
feeding them, patting them.

Perhaps it's our final second,
and the souls are attentive, fixed
on that small living thing.

Something Like

And so the souls came to live
in a country where everything
was something like something else
and nothing was the thing itself.

The sun, for instance
was like a melon someone
had broken open and
put back together again
awkwardly.

And face-like shapes
appeared on a vast scale, but faintly,
as if paint had been applied
to a canvas with something like a sponge.

> At a time resembling afternoon,
> someone like you
> could have a kind of tea
> with someone who was almost
>   a person.

The life of the soul, was it life
itself, or something approximating to it?
At times, it was encouragingly like it.

Strangers

Each soul is a stranger to the other,
as if one were a trapeze artist
and another a refuse collector,
or a museum attendant.
But each contains a definite hint
of the other, as if the trapeze artist
could easily take on the glance
of the refuse collector.
Each soul in its separate guise
passes down the thoroughfare.

When the souls collide,
they are confused because
they cannot easily tell whether
it is themselves or the other
who is the museum attendant.
Some linger on street corners
trying to work it out
with a fine degree of patience –
the customs of the infinite,
and the weather permitting.

The Inspection

Of course, you cannot look at a soul
under a magnifying glass,

but it's tempting to try.
To hold one securely between
your finger and thumb,
taking care not to pinch it.

Lay it on a sheet,
or table-top, and capture it
in an instant when it isn't
folding in on itself.

Suppose the soul's a kind of cloud
somewhere between hyacinth
and grape green, with a rind
like a slice of lemon...

Then suddenly there's no thick lens.
Just your open eyes –
and your peopled life
rising up, as if for an inspection.

And melting quickly away.

Hotel

All those passages and corridors,
deep red walls and indoor rivers.

So what does the soul
think of its temporary home,
the spongy,
        the leaky places
and the heart, like Big Ben
presiding over everything?

Perhaps the soul is drawn
to the body's holes and windows,
knowing that one day
it will surely leave.
Without a backward glance.

Was the body really such a good hotel?

Without Them

The souls often wonder
what we'd be like
without them,
if we'd be able to carry on.

Perhaps we'd invite something else in –
a spool of magnetic tape.
Gravel.
A black sun.

They picture us on the road,
desperate for a lift,
a snack from another planet.
The soulless – stricken like scarecrows.

Intent on startling the seasons away.

Two Dates

There are only two dates: my day of birth, day of death.
FERNANDO PESSOA

Through all our frenetic years
they have no real need for diaries.

The souls carry with them
our first stupendous day –
and leave a space for our unknown last.

Two dates which bind together
our existence.

As soon as they have them both
they'll throw them to the heavens
like confetti.

Ridding themselves of clutter.
Unravelling all our days.

Do They Miss Us?

Eventually, they do.

Not our bodies,
the intricate workings,
the fine limbs – not our minds,
nor even our hearts. Not really
us, but themselves in us –

the souls wriggling into place.
A flame in a gemstone.
A live wire. Truly
we were the great love
of their unfathomable lives.

The Scanner

Who could bear to look at their own soul?
Who could contain their excitement?
Better by far, with a semblance of calm,
to point the scanner at someone else
in the hope of a unique sighting.

Not everyone approves.
And there have been complaints
even from the souls themselves
who beg to be left alone
to do their own thing.

Blameless souls,
swimming in the depths of simplicity!

This Town

This town we think is home,
is somewhere else. Abroad.
Every night we travel
miles and miles to get here,

and if, in the morning, it seems
familiar, that's just
a trick of the light. It isn't
our bedroom, our bedclothes.

Even our breath is scarcely
our own – the souls maintain
they gave it as a gift.
Quite casually.

How did they come to let it go?
Doubtful, we shake our heads.

Delight

Days that we perceive the least
because they flow so fast –

rare days that run like rivers.
The souls wade in, and splash about.

Out There

Most days, the souls
would rather be somewhere else.

Not bottled up,
but out there in a landscape,
under an old oak, by a wood signposted
private, watching the bushes
grow pricklier, wilder, adding
their little bit of transfiguration,
like a shaft of sun through cloud.
Not proprietorial, lordly
in the foreground, like Gainsborough's
Mr and Mrs Andrews,
but merging into the fields –
as one brushstroke disappears into the next.

Ventriloquism

They can't sit us on their knee.
Though when the act is over
it's just as if we're stuffed into a suitcase.

And what about those insinuations?
The repartee from nowhere?
Someone is calling you personally,

from within, from the corner of the room.
Then voices everywhere – in the cellar,
up on the roof.

The souls are determined – practising
ventriloquism as if they had
a larynx, a throat.

More intriguing than the radio,
the telephone – this oracle,
this ceaseless voice.

Yes

Soul mates explode with *yes* –
it isn't a word,
but a gust of air, a volley of light.

They are their own children,
their own parents.
And where is *no*,
that wastrel *no*?

They have taken him
out into the woods
and left him there.

Lovers

Fortunate souls have countless lovers.
The silver birches love them.

The fat sizzling in the pan.
The alphabet loves them, even the rarer letters,

and the vacancies between words.
The heroic titles of books love them.

The doorknobs and switches.
The paint thinner, the smear of apricot jam.

And the bubble harbours rainbow lights
for them and swells like a soul itself,

adored, buoyant, doomed to reach
perfection – just before it bursts.

When We're Very Still

Occasionally, when we're very still,
the souls take fright
and think we've died, anticipate
the loss of a partner.
Like people posing for a photograph,
we're still, before we're stilled.

When we really die, some souls
are traumatised,
and take to drink – those liquids
offered by another world.
So dry they could be
manufactured in the desert.

Back on earth
there's someone missing.

Yet there's so much life
a soul could drown in it.

Trapped

A soul has a horror
of being trapped underground.
So, experimentally
it prepares itself, inhabits
a loaf of bread,
the heart of a stone.

But it can't prepare itself
for the totality – the relentlessness
of soil, the maggots and the grit.
The way, at last, the world
appears, but darker, stuffier –
a subterranean department store.

No windows, no natural light at all.
Caverns, grottos, useless things for sale.

Nothing

'Bring nothing with you' the notice says.
And dutifully the souls shed everything.

But desperately
they gather up nothing and hold it

close to them, as if it were a child.
Nothing is more precious than life,

the souls chant. *Let's dance.*
And then the music stops.

And then they lose their voice.

Eine Kleine Nachtmusik

(after the painting by Dorothea Tanning)

You can lock the doors, even
bolt the air, but there's no way
of keeping your daughters in at night.
It doesn't matter how old they are –
three or four, six or seven –
a tornado throws them down the path
and ravishes them.
Stars glint like metal in their hair.
The darkness, fine as artists' ink,
seeps into their nightclothes.
If you follow them down the path –
you turn to stone.

Then long after the midnight hour
the wind flings them back into the hallway
and up onto the landing
with its cracked green paint.
Their blouses open up like curtains
on their narrow, childish chests.

Your daughters grow giant sunflowers
in the gloom.
Their hair streams upwards
thick as cypress trees.

The Conjurors

How could they have known
that their child would finally arrive
so much more impressively
than a rabbit from a hat,
and then keep on arriving
like the silk scarves
knotted into an endless rope.

Experimentally, playfully
the conjuror-parents had lifted up
their own lives and covered them
with a soft, red cloth, and those
lives had duly vanished,
never to reappear
in the same form, despite

the most theatrical of gestures,
the most solemn incantations.

Her Parents Are Lonely

after all, there are only two of them
on the whole wide earth.
Surely their infant
who is so many weathers,
must have a multitude of parents –

so her mother and father scanned
the horizon searching for the others,
the lost parents of their child.
Perhaps they would drift
across the hills in pairs
at first slowly, then eagerly,

as if glad to have left the ark
and found themselves on dry land.

The Twins

And so the twins were born –
not two infants
but a mother and a father.

Clearly they were not identical,
and they were not inseparable.
But suddenly they shared a birth-time
though they couldn't tell
whether they were years old
or just a second old.

    Often their child filled entirely
    their watchful compound eye.

    Their hands were continually busy
    making a sinewy cat's cradle.
    At times their fingers moved
    in sympathy as if one pair of hands
    was sketching the other.

    And these twins tried to wear
    the same clothes – flecked
    with their shaky authority.

In their darkest hours
they were afraid of falling
through the galaxy,
of snapping apart
at their shiny hinge.

    They were two moons
            two suns
                two trees
    bending over a hammock.
    They were lighter, heavier
    than they'd ever been,
    more hollow and more solid.

And still their single lives continued
like the remnants of a festival
in another town.

The Captain's Child

She moved as if within a circle of sea-air.
Then she stepped outside this private zone
and held it, shrunk small and watery
like a bubble in her hands.

Inside this sphere was a tiny ship
so dazzling, so covered in reflections
its surfaces were hardly visible at all.
She was the captain's child –

and the captain of her ship.

Island Daughter

She plays quietly on the island,
frightened to wake the babies.
A century ago she was an infant herself –

now she's older than her parents.
They watch with her for the signal –
the shooting light in the trees.

Once the sea is certain of her name
she'll leave stealthily
on a raft heaped with everything

she thinks she'll never need,
the sail lashed tightly
to the mast of her childhood.

Turbines

In the end
we were nothing more

and nothing less
than two wind turbines

masking the view,
while our children tore,

shouting, across the wavy
lines of the hills.

We were massive,
the largest in the land.

Starkly visible, we strode
into the sky – then

off the stage completely,
holding in our arms

that rush of air
we tried

to make our own.

Go Back to England

Model Town, Lahore.
I was born there, lived there

briefly.
What was it like?

Nothing like the houses I built
from Lego. Not a bit like

Welwyn Garden City.
But perhaps the houses *were*

spaced out and the gardens tended.
Lemon trees. Not apple trees.

*

In Model Town, the story goes,
to save money,

my mother made my father's
handkerchiefs from his shirt tails.

My mother, newly married
and wrapped in her Englishness,

tried to make herself at home
in her husband's Pakistan.

Cycled along the sweltering lane
to play Mrs Plover's piano.

Sometimes, at night,
the buffaloes wandered in

and grazed on the lawn.
What a noise they made!

She hardly missed Hatfield at all.

*

At least, not until 1954.
What happened then?

Well, I was born –
and the seismic happening

the birth of a child, rocked
everything.

The flat-roofed house trembled,
the grey-green trees shook,

and the ground beneath
my mother's feet gaped.

Kicking above the cracks
was a baby, who wailed,

who detested the heat
and the cold.

It was as if the solid house
had collapsed.

But the earth couldn't swallow up
the baby clinics

because there weren't any,
couldn't swallow up the wise advice

because there wasn't any.
And where was a set of scales

to weigh a baby?

*

So there was my mother – suddenly
thousands of miles from home.

Her phrase book instructed
You must water the plants

while I am away in the hills.
But that was no use at all.

And the lemon trees
were no use at all.

*

Go back to England
said the doctor.

Go back to England
said the stones and boulders.

Go back to England
urged the dusty grass.

*

July gasped in the heat
the day we left Model Town.

My mother hoped to be
a different mother.

The ocean knew
I would be translated

into an English girl.

Model Town: a district of Lahore.

The House with One Window

Things that are too wintry –
like a hole dug in a frozen garden
and darkness falling.
A house with one window.
A smile with the mouth
and not with the eyes.
The muffling of the soul.
Things I shouldn't write about
that dissolve like snowmen
in the rain

*

A first brother –
younger than me.
Eternally young.
And suddenly
I'm in the little house
with one window.

*

I asked
Where is he?
And the answer swooped in –
He's gone on a journey.
Everything in the room
moved fractionally
as if it had gone
on a journey too.
But I couldn't go.
Perhaps because the way was too icy
or too far
like over a mountain range.
Or too adventurous.
Another world.

In this movement
of everything
I was very still.

*

I'd raced across the ward
to visit him –
the lino was so shiny
and slippery I fell.
I'd been walking a year
and it was as if I'd run my first race
on this burnished floor
brown as a conker
wide as a river.
And the cots were there
on the other side –
the bank
just out of reach.
I fell in, my eagerness
swallowed up.
I could have been an adult
feeling shame
at losing control.

The sick-ward had no windows at all.

*

Absence was
an arm where there was no arm
an eye with no colour
no reflections
a smile but no mouth.
And the house more spacious –

no brother.

In a way it was a golden space.
Presence and absence
tried to sit down
and play by the fire.

*

Scarcely more
than a baby myself
I held a baby
inside me
as a camera

might hold inside it
the ghost
of a photograph
or a feather might whisper
the idea of a bird
or a soul might receive
the imprint
of a soul.

*

Hatted and mittened
I am peering into
his Rolls-Royce pram.
His face is broad
as health.
He's wide-mouthed
as if he's smiling
gazing out of the photograph
into my parents' tidied
bedroom –
into the airy
the airless
distance.

*

So what's left?
The bleak force of it all.
And a curious feeling
of balance –
those inner scales.
Sorrow, the exact weight
of love.
Our children
our parents
on loan like library books.

A house with one window
opening, closing, shuttered, opening

The Bells

The streets are well-lit at the heart of the child.
He hasn't seen them yet –
but there are elegant, gracious squares,
shady trees and fountains.
The inhabitants are certain where to go
and newcomers are carefully questioned.

Streets away, at the edge of the suburbs
the lights start to dim
and the trees along the avenues agitate.
People scurry about in confusion
and the roads disappear altogether.
Buildings are ramshackle,
haunted by the derelicts, the isolates.
They have no official papers.

But still the bells ring out
in the elegant squares,
tremendous peals
more than the ear can cope with –
ring out in the heads of the most
unsettling of strangers.

The huge bells of adulthood

The huge bells of childhood

The Boy from Bombay
(for Varuna and Jan)

He sleeps – one fist clenched
on a fragment of India.

Shadow-brothers
moving behind his eyelids
curl up on their low beds
clatter their metal breakfast plates.
A roomful of lost boys.

He wakes to the crisp Swiss air
the clean grey streets
a view of the mountains.
He wakes to new parents.
At last they'd brought him home!

*

The new child with the new name.
Amit André, seeing with his ears
hearing with his eyes,
his present tumbling
over his past and future.
An absence of dust.

A computerised image
of Amit with elephants
announces his arrival.
His forefinger stroking
an immense turquoise forehead.
The boy from Bombay
in loving command
of paper animals.
His eyes watchful
and amazed.

*

Years later, perhaps,
he'll look in the mirror
and picture himself
for a moment
somewhere else.

Not in this town numbed
by snow, but under the yellow
basalt of the Gateway of India.
Or buying pomfret in the market.

*

He strains to see –
as if he could uncover
the full story.
As if he could untie
a boat on the lake,
row it from one world
to another –

backwards and forwards –
through the sunlight
and the shadows.

Flight

What is it about Mohammed Ayaz
that sticks in the mind?

Is it how he squeezed himself
into the wheel bay
   of a Boeing 777,
found somewhere to crouch and cling?

Is it how, at 30,000 ft in the freezing
dark, he turned into a block of ice?

Is it where his twisted body was found,
in a DIY store car park,
   in London,
by a worker – on her way
to load paint tins
   into strong paper bags?

What is it about Mohammed Ayaz
that sticks in the mind?

Is it his foolishness?
Is it his courage?

Is it that his family's debts,
were as high as Mount Mankial?

   Harvesting the onion crop,
   they had so little time to grieve.

Is it that 3,000 people share
only one telephone
in the broad green valley of Swat?

Is it that routinely the captain
opened the undercarriage
and tipped him out?

   And others will fall in this way,
   on almost exactly the same spot.

Allah gives and Allah takes away
said his father.
He was meant to die
at this time.

But the son who had fallen
to earth groaned
It was the wrong time.
The wrong way.

The Tunnel

I was stunned, as anyone would be
to find themselves metamorphosed
into a tunnel, that someone
wanted to get through – but
they couldn't just amble along
or drive straight to the end.

Perspectives were lost.
No daylight could be glimpsed
though red flowers
dripped from the ceiling.

It was part of the earth
but the floor was tender –
you'd have to walk barefoot.
It was very close, very damp.
A passage under the sea,
through the mountains.
And pain chiselling away
with his astonishing tool kit,
his axes and wrenches,
his screwdrivers and his knives.
Busier and busier.

I would have spoken
with my echoey voice.
Calmed the one inside
who was trying to escape
almost against her will.

Sleep, I would say.
Sleep and try again.
The world is waiting.

Enormous

How could it have happened
that she had given birth
to a baby so much bigger than herself?

  She could hardly lift him –
  dragged him onto her bed.

She was the helpless one.
Well-meant words
shrivelled in the air.
Visitors smiled uneasily
as this enormous child,
its head bald as a giant mushroom,
reached out its pudgy hands
into every corner of its mother's life.

  The health visitor threw her graphs
  and charts into the sea.

The woman might have chosen
an infant made of leaves,
or one with lovely cloud formations
passing across his eyes.
Or one who fitted into a walnut shell.

  Stretched and torn,
  stitched, half-mended,
  she sighed and rested her head
  on her baby's broad chest.

The butterflies flew from her stomach,
and perched all over the bed.
How light they were,
how frail and buoyant!

Daddy Goes Hunting

What will Daddy bring back
when he goes hunting?

A woman from the forest
with red-berry lips?

Or perhaps he'll bring back
a rabbit skin –

fur softer than the thought of snow.
Dangerously soft, troubling fur.

He'll rub his bristly face against it
as he rubbed his cheek on our stomachs.

Draw his finger through it,
parting it like a harvester.

He'll not be happy to bring one skin –
he'll bring hundreds, and sew them together

with strong, rough stitches.
Pack the fridge with flesh,

awful and glassy.
Wrap us all in his blanket

until we're so hot we can hardly breathe.
Then we'll drift into sleep, pressing

our lips to tickling fur,
hold sweaty hands under the cover,

dig our chins into each other's chests.
In the morning we'll struggle free,

roll ourselves towards the walls,
while Daddy sets off for work,

banging our concealed front door,
scraping the ice off the windscreen.

Going hunting for a few hours, a few years.
Leaving us with his gunshot.

His promise to return.

Howls

No bricks. We've built our house with howls.
We've lain one howl upon another –
the wind helps us stick them together.

The wolf likes this house that's made of itself.
It crouches in the corner of the sitting-room,
mouth gaping, tongue red as a wound.

It assures us we lead strongly-scented lives.
We pick up each other's smell miles away,
hear each other's voice across the towns.

There's snow on the pine-fringed rug.
Snow on our eyebrows.
We are so very married, but the wolf

is fostering us as if we were its cubs.
His jaw closes on our backs,
leaves no scratch marks on our skin.

He's a surprisingly kind parent.
Plays tig. And tug-of-war.
Brings us bones to throw.

The Nest-Makers

I dreamt I saw the girls in the art room,
their long hair brushing the communal table.
They made wondrous nests in the northern light,
from fabric in spicy shades – coriander
with touches of chilli red and cardamom green –
fine cottons and velvets, torn into strips
and woven into bowls of twigs
and domes of grass. Nests not destined
for holes in trees or the crevices of buildings,
sailed on the table like small craft –
some already carrying their blue-white eggs.

The nest-makers. How to bring them back,
spy on them again, how to make a nest
in the brilliance of night.

In a Railway Carriage

We are alone in the carriage,
filling its narrowness.

He is so keen to hold my hand,
and I am so proud

that the King of Beasts
treats me as his friend.

He waves his paw
on the quiet side of my words,

has no need for lionesses,
spreading trees or reed beds.

Inclining his great head
with its serious mane,

he creates his own dusk.
This lion has singled me out

of the air.
We are contented,

leaning against each other.
The train stops at every station.

The world is too sleepy
to bang on the window.

Of Chairs and Shadows
(for Eileen Hogan)

When we tire of one another's conversation
it is such a relief

to let the chairs and shadows
take over in their unobtrusive way.

But they are not so quiet.
Chairs will converse with the walls,

the rugs, though chiefly
they're interested in their own shadows.

It's an uneasy relationship –
shadows are in love with themselves,

and so are chairs.
The shadow teases the chair mercilessly –

You are here. No, you were here.
I can help you to be more.

No, help you to be less.
Sometimes they do seem to speak in unison,

both daring to interrupt the light.
The chair boasts of its personality.

The shadow is neither impressed
nor unimpressed.

Shadows are beyond all this.
Both know when something momentous

is happening – could it be
the soul of a chair has been repaired?

Has there been a change in the room's
slow, bright, geometric dance?

What are shadows made of?
Ghosts, or smoke?

They throw their sharp,
their tender nets –

and we are caught like fish.

HOW THE STONE
FOUND ITS VOICE

(2005)

HOW THE STONE FOUND ITS VOICE

How the World Split in Two

Was it widthways or lengthways,
a quarrel with the equator?
Did the rawness of the inside sparkle?

Only this is true:
there was an arm on one side
and a hand on the other,
a thought on one side
and a hush on the other.

And a luminous tear
carried on the back of a beetle
went backwards and forwards
from one side to the other.

How the Countries Slipped Away

Beneath their covering of prayers and exhalations,
boasts and dreams, the countries
were preparing to slip away, to part from
their iron reserves, their megastores, their temples
and their palaces, their rivers and valleys,
to forsake their courts of law, their summer resorts,
their uranium mines, their health farms.

Almost imperceptibly the countries slipped away –
clinging to their photographs, the homesick knew
there was no point looking for them.

How the Answers Got Their Questions

The most difficult task of all was not
finding new questions or harder questions,
dipping your wrists into the blood of questions.

It was finding questions for the answers
which had none, prising them out of the earth,
catching them before they burst into flames.

How the City Lost Its Colour

Just one bang – and the colour fled.
Eyes lost their gemlike lustre, their depth.

The lions in the zoo were separated from their tawniness
which hung above them, then vanished completely.

The purple stole away from the skins of plums,
and buildings were stripped of their warmer hues.

A vision which might have had a dash of aquamarine
was suddenly bereft.

Neither artists nor scientists could replicate
the earth's glowing subtleties.

What was the colour of hope? How to remember it?

How the Animals Tried on Our Clothes

And finally, after meeting upon meeting
there wasn't one creeping, crawling or galloping thing
that didn't yearn to be in our place, to stroll about
in our clothes under the changing skies, to ruminate,
and to gather all thoughts into a fiery ball.

But the problem was our skin,
which seemed at once too thick and too thin.
And that plucked look, that repellent smoothness!
With relief they slipped back into their fur
and feathers. Even scales were a comfort.

How the Sky Got a Hole in It

Nobody knew how it happened, yet there it was,
a gaping hole with torn, crinkled edges –
you couldn't look up at the sky without seeing it.

There was no method of patching it up, or filling it in,
or softening it, no way to cope with the pain caused by
the merest upward glance to where, in the clearest blue,

the sun and the hole vied for attention.

How the Words Feared the Mouth

Some words lay quietly,
they didn't wish to be roused,

while others were restless,
waiting for the drama to begin.

Sensitive words feared the mouth –
that slash in the face, the hole

which could fill with potatoes and beer.
Half-formed words were often lost.

And others were equally unfortunate –
it was their fate

to be cruelly nailed to the air.

How a Long Way Off Rolled Itself Up

Once, there was a place called A Long Way Off –
it was too far away to contemplate.

All that was known
was that the grass was a strange texture,
the trees grew upside down, and the houses
appeared to have been turned inside out.

So people were unprepared
when A Long Way Off rolled itself up
and edged a little nearer, and kept on
moving, until it had ventured so close
you could smell it, and breathe in
its otherness.

People laughed uneasily. A Long Way Off
was close enough to singe their hair.

How the Children Were Born

Doctors and midwives were aghast.
There, embedded in each infant palm
was the barrel of a tiny gun.

Babies had always raged – but
could any child be born knowing,
and prepared for war?

Enmity was handed down
like an heirloom.
The guns grew with the babies,
poking like bone through the soft skin.

How Thought Accompanied the Traveller

Thought tried to go everywhere with the traveller,
across the treacherous borders, into remote
villages where strangers were scarcely seen.

It could be brazen, pushing itself into nightclubs
and brothels, struggling with unwelcoming places,
taking a deep breath and squeezing itself in.

And thought could become as capacious
as a country which opens its doors hospitably
to the adventurous, or the destitute.

It could shrink to the size of a quiet town,
then without warning trek off into the outback.
So there was a tension between the traveller

and itinerant thought, although often
they appeared to be the perfect companions.

How Yesterday Joined Today and Tomorrow

At first there was no yesterday.
There was today and tomorrow
and there was long ago,

but nobody wanted to look at
the details of the day before.
Sometimes the brightness was

too much, shining in their eyes,
or the newness was a problem
like paint not yet dry.

Then people became braver
and examined that parcel of time –
viewed it in all its rawness.

Yesterday was always somewhere
tinged with sadness.
Long ago was inviolate –

yesterday fell to the enemy
again and again.

How the Stone Found Its Voice

We had waited through so many lifetimes
for the stone to speak, wondered if

it would make compelling pronouncements,
anything worth writing down.

Then after the war of wars
had ground to a shattering halt, the stone

emitted a small grinding sound rather like
the clearing of a throat.

Let us be indifferent to indifference,
the stone said.

And then the world spoke.

Half-and-Half

The thin line running from my navel downwards
meant, I thought, that I was half-and-half,

like the coffee my mother drank in restaurants.
That was sophisticated –

but to be half-and-half oneself? And one part
stemmed from a country that wasn't whole –

West and East Pakistan, on different sides
of the pendulous India, because powerful people

had carved up the world like the Sunday joint.
Pakistan belonged to the politicians, the priests.

And to my geography teacher who leapt across
ditches on field trips, and enlightened me

briskly as to where I was born.
Discomfited, I put the pin on the map.

The Suits

My father's forties' suit, bought when he first came to England,
pin-striped with broad lapels, comfortingly chocolate, but crisp.

He and his Pakistani friends and their we-have-arrived-suits.
In a black-and-white snap, Dad sits on the grass at a rural crossroads,

head in his hands, signs pointing in all directions: Digswell, Welwyn,
Tewin Wood... Even here, deep in the countryside, he's wearing

his suit. *He's handsome as a doctor*, our neighbour said.
My father and his friends, marvelled at wherever they went, ordering

a sandwich at the Comet Hotel, or shopping on the Barnet bypass.
This was before *Go back home!* Their suits of armour

could have stood up without them. Walked on and on.

Ghosts

My mother's father refused
to attend my parents' marriage.
But it's hard not to see him
at the wedding breakfast,
more hauntingly present
for his absence – a pale ghost,
uncertain, disapproving,
then muttering *I'm not going.*
My grandfather, surrounded
by multitudes of other wraiths
from the box of the English family,
all frowning on this union of East
and West, swelling the numbers –
it became the hugest wedding ever.
My grandmother was there,
and so was my grandfather's sister,
fighting a brave path through
the ghosts, raising the shining
clarity of their glasses.

Spit

I'm back in Oxford, summer '72 –
my father's aspirations thirty years ago.
A family visit. Sun and cloud.
Girls in floating Laura Ashley dresses,
climbing into student cars, driven
to picnics, to who knew where.
The shining ones – could I really
become one of them?
Then cutting through all this,
a man steps forward, spits at us,
and hurries on – revealing
my mother and father to me,
stripped of their protective glass,
their two colours, like those double
erasers we used then, for ink and pencil.
My parents, fixed, momentarily
in that hallowed city
of pavements, noise and clouds.
My mother's furious face,
my father's seeming absentmindedness.
Little said. The moving on.

English Roses

What drew Harinder to the rose gardens?
Was it a Pakistani's love for English girls,
ladies of consequence, superior women?

Thick gloves dealt with their thorns,
and thankfully they had no voice,
just opened their white, their lilac hearts,
displayed themselves like eager debutantes.

Nurturing such women, spraying their greenfly,
was a serious matter, like cutting off heads.
He called them by their names –
                              and they responded.

Penelope, Emily Gray, Ena Harkness...
In the ordered, windy nurseries
so many of them chose him.

So Much Goes On

(after Jean Rhys)

It seems to me that Englishmen
make love with all their clothes on –
they think it more respectable that way.

And then, of course, for luck they add
a macintosh, to keep the dark rain off.
Under an umbrella, so much goes on.

England, I Am Gazing at Your Body

stretched out on the sea,
buoyed up on the waves.
I watch it brighten and darken,
go warm and cold.

Weakened, shrunk, thrown back
on my mercy, you ask for a grain
of understanding –
all I can do is sniff you, your industrial belts,
your hedgerows, your crags and reservoirs,
rest an elbow on a grass roundabout.

I press the weight of my body
against the bulk of yours.
The wind blows across our contours,
the black-dog rocks, the winking lights,
the peopled parks, an unforgiving street.

England, it's time
                        to call the children in.

I pull myself off you.
Hard to prise my stickiness from yours.

Rural Scene

The luminous Norfolk skies,
the tractors, the gunshots,
the still ponds, the darting rabbits,
cow parsley by the field gates –

all are re-imagining themselves
because Tariq walks in his village,
part of the scene, yet conspicuous,
as if he is walking a tiger.

Alamgir Hashmi's Camel

I want to borrow Hashmi's camel,
that formed itself
from an American cloud,
its hump
the difficult curve
of the earth.

I wonder if it's on loan
for border crossings, awkward journeys,
for travelling in English deserts.

Let me welcome it,
shy from early persecution,
a little grumpy
despite its many advantages,
introduce it to our neighbourhood.

I turn my head
and sand blows past the houses,
swirls down the streets and avenues.
The camel closes its nostrils.

These are heated times.
It treats the boating-lake
as its water-hole.

A number of residents
have not wished for
a black or brown person
as a neighbour.

And now they have a camel
suggesting itself as a means of transport,
a beast with coarse hair
and a tufted tail,
a lofty expression
and nothing particular to do.

It is trying to sum something up,
to get a feel for the suburbs,
its hump full of unfamiliar words
and disturbing customs.

It moves with a swaying stride,
kneels by the Mace shop.
England, a new thought on its lips.

Shift

This is what the peasants in the Punjab
ate for lunch. We're puzzled –

cold salmon, coleslaw, lettuce?
Bread and onions, he says, launching

a memory across the dining-table.
I try to grasp it, and swiftly

the walls fall back: that village
off the Grand Trunk Road we stopped at

on the bus. Misted green and gold.
Women toiling, marooned in the fields.

Old men on low beds, napping in the shade
while barefoot children gather round us,

nets of holes for vests. *Bread and onions*,
he repeats. That sweet, sharp shift

of place and time. That jolt, and then
we're here. We're back.

For My Daughter

Your name rests for a moment on my tongue
and speaks resoundingly of Englishness.
I let it stay a little longer

and it swells and fluctuates.
You are here with a whisper
of another continent in your bones,

though you can't yet think of it like that.
And perhaps we are all immigrants
in these towns and villages,

and all strangers to ourselves.
When I say your name it melts like ice,
or starts to grow –

a hospital, a playground,
a path through the fields, the sky.

Homesick for the Earth

(after Jules Supervielle)

One day we'll say 'The sun ruled then.
Don't you remember how it shone on the twigs,
on the old, as well as the wide-eyed young?
It knew how to make all things vivid
the second it alighted on them.
It could run just like the racehorse.
How can we forget the time we had on Earth?
If we dropped a plate it clattered.
We'd look around like connoisseurs,
alert to the slightest nuance of the air,
knew if a friend was coming towards us.
We'd pick daffodils, collect pebbles, shells,
but we couldn't catch the smoke.
Now smoke is all we hold in our hands.'

Whisper in Agony

(after Jules Supervielle)

No need to be shocked.
Close your eyelids until
they harden into stone.

Disregard your heart
even if it stops.
It only beats for itself
on its private slope.

Your hands will stretch out
in their boats of ice
and your forehead will be blank
as a vast empty square
that separates two armies.

Movement

(after Jules Supervielle)

The horse that turned its head,
saw what no one has ever seen,
then carried on grazing
in the shade of the eucalyptus.

It wasn't a person or a tree.
It wasn't a mare,
nor even a memory of the wind
exercising in the foliage.

It's what another horse
suddenly turned its head
and glimpsed at that same hour
twenty thousand centuries ago,

and what no being will see again,
not man, horse, fish, insect –
until the soil is reduced
to a crumbled statue
without arms, legs or head.

Besieged

(after Jules Supervielle)

The great bulk of the mountain hesitates at my window

How can a mountain get in with its height,
its boulders and pebbles – a piece of the Earth
in conflict with the sky?

My house is surrounded by woods

Do the woods have a say indoors?
Can our branches, our leafy world
influence this room with its white bed,
tall candlestick, flowers drenched in a vase?
What can a wood do for a man, walled in,
who rests his writing hand on his arm?
Let's consider our delicate roots.
The man hasn't seen them, he peers
into his depths, looking for trees
at the back of his tongue.

And the river says

I have no interest in men or women,
I flow for myself.
I am never where you expect to find me.
I outrun myself, can't bear to stand still.
I pity those who rush off on two legs –
they never fail to retrace their steps.

But the star murmurs to itself

I shiver on the end of a thread –
if no one's thinking of me I cease to exist.

Riderless Horses

(after Jules Supervielle)

Once there was a cavalry troop,
long dispersed.
The horses would soak their necks in the future
so they could gallop on and on.

They were wild and tireless.

Sleek black, alarming,
they'd run in all directions,
spin round in circles,
stopping only to die,
change pace in the dust, and start again.

The frantic colts would catch up with the mares.

So many horses have passed this way
and nothing is left of them
but the beating of their hooves.

Let me listen to the hoof beats of my past –
my former heart beating in its glade.

And let the heart I'm stuck with now
give way, drunk – with the brevity of life.

School Closure

That day I set off for school in the surprising calf-deep snow,
the road spun into a field extending like the inexpressible –
I stood out with each of the solid others, the town no more
than a grey-white backdrop – and school at the end

of the long trudge like a shelter for animals in lined coats,
but turning us away, letting us loose because there was
to be no school. The rock of the place suddenly fractured.
It was the lost clue to our existence.

A Turn of the Screw

Suppose we were both ghosts
climbing out onto a tower
on a moonlit evening –

children all over the land
in bed or delaying bedtime,
asking for drinks of water,

or one more story, then
imagining the wardrobe
as something else –

parent ghosts,
clinging to a turret,
an architectural oddity,

in sight of a stranger
who rounds the bend
stops on the path.

When you are dead,
our little girl asks,
can I live in your house?

Colposcopy

Try climbing a hill in October
and peering across to the Spring.

Can you leap from one season to the next?
Is there time to practise?

                    *

I could trace this back
through all the colours of the spectrum.
Did I become a woman
inch by inch?

The nurse says 'Don't worry.'
Worry is a swollen word –
no box around it.

                    *

The leaflet is blue as a summer's day,
each word flawless,
drawing strength from the others,
kind and clear and stripped of their drama.

Does the test hurt?

Colposcopy – a tricky name.
Hard to enunciate, hard to remember.
This treatment is a minor procedure.

                    *

A close examination,
closer than you could ever get to yourself.
A fearful intimacy
like marriage to a stranger.

Each minute, a cell.

You will not stay overnight.
The night will wait up for you elsewhere.

*

Some women find the test an unpleasant experience.

Others consider it a kind of party,
take a balloon and wear an animal mask.

*

Open out the leaflet –
a slope turns into a widow's peak
or a little blue hill.

Early detection is best.

*

In a room with no outlook
my half-known body, packed
with pleasure and displeasure,
will surrender its information.

The magnified view.

Picnic

It's a cone biopsy. Or a picnic in the sky.
The women lie around with their legs in the air
and the doctor and nurses drift in on clouds.
The women lie back and lie back – they
hadn't realised how far back they could go.
But still the scalpel hops towards them.

Hops and flies of its own accord,
quicker, knowing exactly where it's going.
The women float away from the paper cloth
the clean white picnic plates. The scalpel
has a tiny beak to peck at the women
who hide at the back of the sky

where the weather comes from.
The uncertain weather.

The Thieves

A period, you'd imagine, is no use
to anyone, but the woman who owns it,
who thought she held it secure

in the safe of her body.
Yet thieves broke in and grabbed it,
took it instead of her jewellery:

She's forty-nine, she won't miss it –
we'll just take one, maybe two.
On the other hand, we'll have the lot,

stash them away. Nothing to boast about.
Not anything you'd forget, though.
To make off with them on a quiet night –

it's like stealing the darkness itself,
or taking the moon, bowling it away,
expecting it to retain its glow.

Spanish Birdsong

Squeakier, like the waves themselves
squeaking against each other
wailing over a lost message.

Suddenly, my father
didn't make it here,
could hardly walk the long
journey from the chair
to the door.

You could catch a bus,
a distance like that.

My parents' home
from home. Their Spain.

Apartment blocks
rise up behind the beach
like concrete legs.
Spain blocking off Spain.
Legs with balconies,
and with no relation
to each other.

The unidentified birds are here
with their invisible instruments,
acute, cross-shaped birds.
The sky is their canvas –
but it's too large for them.

A gust of Mediterranean air
heads straight for the lacy tablecloth.
It's there in my mother's absence,
along with the plump golden ashtray
in eternal readiness. And our books:
Ballard's *Super-Cannes*,
Milly-Molly-Mandy,
Group Analysis (S.H. Foulkes).

A parental presence weaves
around the Brandy of Jerez,
the cocktail sticks, two ornate
Spanish mirrors, the representations
of an Indian village – yoked oxen,
a girl with a pitcher of water.

The birds (animated black cut-outs)
make a Symphony of Thousands –
a fabulous meshing
above the coastal garden.

Heat builds up on the Explanada d'Espãna,
on the road to Campello
where my father isn't walking.

Up here (Escalera 3)
a little air circulates.
The tablecloth breathes as if inspired.
The white breath of life.

Campello Dawn

At this instant the sea has a subtle sheen like the material for a generous, half-lit blue dress, but with a fault running through it, a darker band, and the sky appears slightly septic above the ballpoint line that separates it from its close yet radically different partner. Hope and pressure – though you try not to think of it like this.

To the innocent eye the crescent moon is positioned differently, rests like a charming boat on a sea without waves. The darkness lifts so swiftly, even as you write a word, let alone put on the kettle with the foghorn whistle. Odd how as the sea lightens its clamour increases until it is fully cacophonous, sounds mad to the point of being hospitalised. You can't compete with such transitions, this darkness lifting and falling as if controlled by someone who thinks quickly.

Spanish Sunrise

This morning I seek the King of Stars
behind grey eucalyptus leaves and watch it
burst leonine through the topmost twigs.
A coin that could buy the world. Ray Bradbury's

description is a good one, yet this morning
it seems reductive. The sun is a complex gift,
suiting the giver – it is generally agreed,
even in Spain, that the sky chose well.

My Father Has Always Loved Marmalade

Now, shrunken he struggles inside the jar –
at his age he has such difficulty making progress.
With his stick he pushes coarse amber shreds
to the side, tries to force a path through
the glowing jelly – to my mother who's faintly
busy at the base of the jar. There's nothing
to get hold of – just this soft stickiness
clogging up the fingers, encasing legs,
and the overpowering marmalade smell.
They can't read a newspaper here,
watch the cricket or entertain friends.
They can't see very much at all
through the smeared glass. But still
the eternal glow – the closeness
of the orange world towards
the end of life.

Castaway

(after Jules Supervielle)

A table quite near to us and a faraway lamp
can't be linked up again in the hostile air.
And right up to the skyline – an empty beach.
A man in the sea is waving, screaming *Help!*
and his echo replies *What do you mean by that?*

Night Visitor

(after Jules Supervielle)

In precarious rooms, I placed a foot on the exact
spot where I thought I'd know everything,

and waited a long time – simply couldn't move.
It was almost daybreak when someone approached.

Could it be the Night herself – this desirable woman
who trembled like a partridge in the sun?

Ill at ease in her own skin,
she wandered about inside herself, inside her heart.

Trying to convince her I was there, I stayed still,
but even my silence stopped short of her.

Her dark gestures, like her constant murmuring,
flew at me from all sides.

When the daylight faded she walked away
with human footsteps, permanently deceived –

to turn up again at the end of the street,
suffering from vertigo, indistinct.

Every night it was the same.
She covered herself with eyes like blind stars.

And since then I have drawn comfort
from my shadows.

The Photographed Hands

(after Jules Supervielle)

They were made to feel at ease in a world of smooth surfaces
where the craggiest mountains are gentle to touch
and can be held in the hollow of a hand.
They were being treated like a face
for the first time in their lives – under the floodlights
they sensed they had a kind of forehead,
and the signs of features being born.
Memory was moving towards this new territory
like a great wave calmly gathering itself.
The consciousness of the brain
reached down to the thumb –
the thumb surrendered lightly.
And while the exposure lasted, the hands
gave a name to the sun, to the beauty of the day.
They found a word for their slight hesitation,
called it 'trembling'
and knew that it came from the human heart
where their warm veins led.
They understood that life passes and is a fragile thing.
Then the floodlights were withdrawn, leaving the hands
with no hint of what they'd gleaned
during that short time with the forces of light.
Though no one by then could even call them forgetful.

The Child on the Stairs
(after Jules Supervielle)

I hear you running up and down the stairs,
but the minute I grab hold of the banister
you turn your face the other way.
I'm convinced you're my childhood
haunting a favourite place.
You hide from me, embarrassed,
but I was a kind of lodger in your house,
so now I can't help recognising you,
even though you make yourself invisible.
You prowl around me when no one's looking,
and hurry away, as from an illicit meeting.
Okay, I won't let on I know you,
but you must also keep our secret –
this constant patter of my early footsteps
on the present-day stairs.

INDEX

INDEX OF TITLES

Titles of poems are shown in roman type, titles of sequences in italics.

9 781852 248024